FAMOUS
FIRST IMPRESSIONS

FAMOUS
FIRST IMPRESSIONS

The Power of Perfect Opening Lines

PAUL VOLPONI

BLOOMSBURY ACADEMIC
NEW YORK · LONDON · OXFORD · NEW DELHI · SYDNEY

BLOOMSBURY ACADEMIC
Bloomsbury Publishing Inc, 1385 Broadway, New York, NY 10018, USA
Bloomsbury Publishing Plc, 50 Bedford Square, London, WC1B 3DP, UK
Bloomsbury Publishing Ireland, 29 Earlsfort Terrace, Dublin 2, D02 AY28, Ireland

BLOOMSBURY, BLOOMSBURY ACADEMIC and the Diana logo
are trademarks of Bloomsbury Publishing Plc

First published in the United States of America 2025

Copyright © Paul Volponi, 2025

Cover images:
© istock/Ola-Ola, © istock/chipstudio, © istock/rangepuppies, © istock/sx70

All rights reserved. No part of this publication may be: i) reproduced or transmitted in any form, electronic or mechanical, including photocopying, recording or by means of any information storage or retrieval system without prior permission in writing from the publishers; or ii) used or reproduced in any way for the training, development or operation of artificial intelligence (AI) technologies, including generative AI technologies. The rights holders expressly reserve this publication from the text and data mining exception as per Article 4(3) of the Digital Single Market Directive (EU) 2019/790.

Bloomsbury Publishing Inc does not have any control over, or responsibility for, any third-party websites referred to or in this book. All internet addresses given in this book were correct at the time of going to press. The author and publisher regret any inconvenience caused if addresses have changed or sites have ceased to exist, but can accept no responsibility for any such changes.

A catalog record for this book is available from the Library of Congress

ISBN: HB: 979-8-8818-0361-2
ePDF: 979-8-7651-6515-7
epub: 979-8-8818-0362-9

Typeset by Susan Ramundo
Printed and bound in the United States of America

For product safety related questions contact productsafety@bloomsbury.com.

To find out more about our authors and books
visit www.bloomsbury.com and sign up for our newsletters.

CONTENTS

Introduction   xiii

1 SETTING, MOOD, AND TONE   1
Dark and Stormy: Charles M. Schulz and Snoopy ("World Famous Author"); Madeleine L'Engle, *A Wrinkle in Time*; Edward Bulwar-Lytton, *Paul Clifford*   1
A Talking Raven: Edgar Allan Poe, "The Raven"   3
Another Starry Night: Don McLean, "Vincent"   4

2 IDENTITY   7
Woman Powered: Taylor Swift, "Blank Space"; Billie Eilish and Finneas O'Connell, "What Was I Made For?"; Olivia Rodrigo, "Jealousy, Jealousy"; Maya Angelou, "Phenomenal Woman"   7
What's in a Name—or Not?: Herman Melville, *Moby-Dick; or, The Whale*   10
Have a Chocolate?: Eric Roth, *Forrest Gump*; Winston Groom, *Forrest Gump*   11
Can You See Me?: Ralph Ellison, *Invisible Man*   13
Nobody Is Somebody: Emily Dickinson, "I'm Nobody! Who Are You?"   15

3 THE HUMAN CONDITION   17
Why Shakespeare?   17
Hamlet's Dilemma: William Shakespeare, *The Tragedy of Hamlet, Prince of Denmark*   18
Songs of Social Change: Marvin Gaye, "What's Going On"; Jay-Z, "Some How Some Way"   19
Warning Signs: Dr. Seuss, *The Butter Battle Book*   21
Mob Mentality: Shirley Jackson, "The Lottery"   22

	You Can Do It Too	23
	A Need to Communicate: Anne Frank, *The Diary of a Young Girl*	24
	The Plight of Addiction: Pink, "Sober"; Selena Odom, "My Master"; Amy Winehouse, "Rehab"; Stephen King; Neil Young, "The Needle and the Damage Done"	25
4	**SELF-DETERMINATION**	**29**
	Making Your Own Way: Lin-Manuel Miranda, *Hamilton*	29
	Change by Example: Michael Jackson, Glen Ballard, and Siedah Garrett, "Man in the Mirror"; Michael Jackson and Lionel Richie, "We Are the World"	31
	From Behind Bars: Dr. Martin Luther King Jr., "Letter from a Birmingham Jail"	33
	The Trap of Hatred: Wendell Berry, "Enemies"	34
	Double Standard: Gwen Stefani and Tom Dumont, "I'm Just a Girl"; Beyoncé Knowles-Carter, "If I Were a Boy"	34
5	**TIME AND SPACE**	**37**
	To Boldly Go: Gene Roddenberry and William Shatner, *Star Trek*; Patrick Stewart, *Star Trek: The Next Generation*	37
	From Science Fiction to Reality: Neil Armstrong, "One Small Step for Man"	38
	May the Force Be with You: George Lucas, *Star Wars*	38
	Space Parody?: Mel Brooks, *Spaceballs*	40
	AI Gone Wrong: Arthur C. Clarke and Stanley Kubrick, *2001: A Space Odyssey*	40
	Hitchhiking: Douglas Adams, *The Hitchhiker's Guide to the Galaxy*	41
	Better Read or Else: Damon Knight, "To Serve Man"; Rod Serling, *The Twilight Zone*	42
	Warring Worlds: H. G. Wells, *The War of the Worlds*	43
	Public Panic: H. G. Wells, "The War of the Worlds"	44
6	**THE ROAD, STREETS, AND OTHER TRAVELS**	**45**
	Nothing to Hide: John Steinbeck, *The Grapes of Wrath*	45

The Boss Voices Tom: Bruce Springsteen, "The Ghost of Tom Joad"	46
Nobody Street: Octavio Paz, "The Street"	47
You Decide: Robert Frost, "The Road Not Taken"	48
Changing Course: Adele and Greg Kurstin, "I Drink Wine"	49
They're Your Footsteps: Walt Whitman, "Song of the Open Road"	50
On the Wind, You Say?: Bob Dylan, "Blowin' in the Wind"	51

7 SPORTS 53

Attention Getting: Jim McKay, *Wide World of Sports*	53
LaPoem James: Sean Thomas Dougherty, "Biography of LeBron as Ohio"	54
Remember When?: John Updike, "Ex-Basketball Player"	56
Surf's Up!: Susan Orlean, "Life's Swell"	57
Wide Shoulders: Ernest Lawrence Thayer, "Casey at the Bat"	58
A Price to Pay?: Eva Holland, "Why We Play"	60
Fighter, Defender, and Advocate: Muhammad Ali, "I Am America"	61
Right Field Is for Heroes: Peter, Paul, and Mary, "Right Field"	62
No-Nonsense Conscience: Sherman Alexie, "Victory"	63

PIT STOP 1: Reflecting on What You've Seen and What's to Come, Plus Potential Projects 65

8 FREEDOM AND CAPTIVITY, SUPERS AND SLEUTHS 67

Freedom and Captivity	67
A Jury of Your Peers?: Reginald Rose, *Twelve Angry Men*	67
Chains of the Mind: Bob Marley, "Redemption Song"	69
Broken and Transformed: Franz Kafka, "In the Penal Colony"	69
Bug Off!: Franz Kafka, *The Metamorphosis*	70
Separate and Unequal: Maya Angelou, "Caged Bird"	71
Life on the Inside: Stephen King, *Rita Hayworth and Shawshank Redemption*; Frank Darabont, *The Shawshank Redemption*	72
Proper Manners and Penance: Langston Hughes, "Thank You, M'am"	73

Supers and Sleuths	74
Revised Steel: Jerome Siegel and Joe Shuster, Superman	75
A Dark Crusader: Bob Kane and Bill Finger, Batman	75
Opening the Door Wider: William Moulton Marston, Wonder Woman	76
Web Slinger: Stan Lee and Steve Ditko, Spider-Man	77
Hey, Sherlock: Arthur Conan Doyle, *A Study in Scarlet* and *The Sign of the Four*	77
Encyclopedia B.: Donald Sobol, *Encyclopedia Brown Gets His Man*	78
Teen Sleuths: Edward Stratemeyer, the Hardy Boys and Nancy Drew	79

9 TRUE LOVE AND HEARTBREAK — 81

Feuding Families: William Shakespeare, *The Tragedy of Romeo and Juliet*	81
Streetlight Serenade: Mark Knopfler, "Romeo and Juliet"	82
Fairy-Tale Romance: Taylor Swift, "I Knew You Were Trouble"	83
Did He or Didn't He?: "Once upon a Time"	84
Love without Obligation: John Hartford, "Gentle on My Mind"	84
Love and Marriage: Jane Austen, *Pride and Prejudice*	85
Can't You Hear Me?: Donika Ross Kelly, "Love Poem: Mermaid"	86
Hold Nothing Back: Janis Ian, "At Seventeen"	87
Constantly Parodied: Elizabeth Barrett Browning, "How Do I Love Thee?"; Karen McCullah and Kristen Smith, *10 Things I Hate about You*	88

10 ORATORS AND FAMOUS SPEECHES — 91

Galvanizing Words: Abraham Lincoln, Gettysburg Address	91
Liberty or Death: Patrick Henry, Speech at Second Virginia Convention	93
A Declaration: Thomas Jefferson, Declaration of Independence	93
The Voice of Youth: Malala Yousafzai, Speech at the United Nations Youth Assembly	94

I Have a Dream: Martin Luther King Jr., "I Have a Dream"   95

No More, Forever: Chief Joseph of the Nez Perce, Surrender Speech   96

Heating Things Up: Greta Thunberg, Speech at the United Nations' Climate Action Summit   97

Heartfelt Farewell: Lou Gehrig, Retirement Speech   98

11   PERSPECTIVE   101

Just Imagine: John Lennon and Yoko Ono, "Imagine"   101

Scrambled Eggs: The Beatles, "Yesterday"   102

The Best and Worst: Charles Dickens, *A Tale of Two Cities*   103

A More Personal Perspective: Billy Joel, "Summer, Highland Falls"   104

Two for One: Mark Twain, *Adventures of Huckleberry Finn*   105

Scrub a Word: Mark Twain, *Adventures of Huckleberry Finn*   106

Blind Faith: Amiri Baraka, "Preface to a Twenty Volume Suicide Note"   107

Parallel Play: Stephen Schwartz, "What Is This Feeling?"   108

Slipper Trivia: *The Wonderful Wizard of Oz*   109

Measure of a Year: Jonathan Larson, "Seasons of Love"   110

12   YOUNG ADULTS   113

Unfortunately Intriguing: Daniel Handler (Lemony Snicket), *A Series of Unfortunate Events*   113

Almost Never: J. M. Barrie, *Peter and Wendy*   114

Missing Parents   115

Angst Personified: J. D. Salinger, *The Catcher in the Rye*   116

The Anti-Holden (Save Ferris!): John Hughes, *Ferris Bueller's Day Off*   116

Modeled Upon: Dav Pilkey, *Captain Underpants: The First Epic Movie*   117

Harry Is Still Harry: J. K. Rowling, *Harry Potter and the Philosopher's Stone*   118

Not So Wimpy: Jeff Kinney, *Diary of a Wimpy Kid*   119

Always Online: T. M. Anderson, *Feed*   120

PIT STOP 2: Reflecting on What We've Seen and What's to Come and More Potential Projects — 123

13 THE SENSES AND UNITY AND DISCORD — 125
   The Senses — 125
   Alphabet Soup: Mark Strand, "Eating Poetry" — 125
   Speaking Up: Paul Simon, "The Sound of Silence" — 126
   Deep Breaths: William Carlos Williams, "Smell!" — 127
   Beyond Us: Judith Wright, "Five Senses" — 128
   You Fill Up My Senses: John Denver, "Annie's Song" — 129
   Unity and Discord — 130
   Love Light: Hafiz, "Even after All This Time" — 130
   The Price and Reward: Rose Marie Juan-austin, "Poetry Is a Solitary Art" — 131
   Sharing the Load: Bill Withers, "Lean on Me" — 132
   Island or Continent: John Donne, *Devotions upon Emergent Occasions* — 133
   Closing the Circle: Jerry Seinfeld and Larry David, *Seinfeld* — 134

14 FANTASY — 137
   Sneak Peak: Stephenie Meyer, *Twilight* — 137
   Toll Taker: Norton Juster, *The Phantom Tollbooth* — 138
   Storm on the Horizon: Rick Riordan, *The Lightning Thief* — 139
   Rabbit Hole: Lewis Carroll, *Alice's Adventures in Wonderland* — 140
   Allusions to Alice: Grace Slick, "White Rabbit" — 141
   Buttercup and Westley: William Goldman, *The Princess Bride* — 141
   Hobbits and Rings: J. R. R. Tolkien, *The Hobbit* and *The Lord of the Rings* — 143

15 THE NATURAL (UNNATURAL) WORLD AND LIFE AND DEATH — 147
   Genesis: The Book of Genesis — 147
   The Lamb and the Tyger: William Blake, *Songs of Innocence* and *Songs of Experience* — 147
   The Creature: Mary Shelley, *Frankenstein; Or, The Modern Prometheus* — 149

Digging Deep: Ada Limón, "Notes on the Below" — 150
Never-Ending Summer: William Shakespeare, "Shall I Compare Thee to a Summer's Day?" — 152
Murdering Sleep: William Shakespeare, *The Tragedy of Macbeth* — 152
Middle of the Night: Dana Gioia, "Insomnia" — 154
Clinging to Light: Dylan Thomas, "Do Not Go Gentle into That Good Night" — 155
Revisiting Emily: Emily Dickinson, "I Heard a Fly Buzz" — 156
Graveyard Ballad: Tom T. Hall, "Ballad of Forty Dollars" — 157
Debating an Ending: Robert Frost, "Fire and Ice" — 158

16 SOCIETY AND ITS INFLUENCES — 161

Three the Easy Way/Hard Way: F. Scott Fitzgerald, *The Great Gatsby*; Lorde, "Royals"; Frederick Douglass, *Narrative of the Life of Frederick Douglass, an American Slave* — 161
Privilege: Plus or Handicap?: Jimmy Page and Robert Plant, "Stairway to Heaven"; Langston Hughes, "Mother to Son" — 164
The Burden of Fame: Bernie Taupin and Elton John, "Candle in the Wind" and "Candle in the Wind 1997"; Eminem, "Stan" — 166
That Book Is Fire!: Ray Bradbury, *Fahrenheit 451* — 168

17 WAR — 171

Heavy Jacket: Gustav Hasford, Michael Herr, and Stanley Kubrick, *Full Metal Jacket* — 171
War and Laughs: Larry Gelbart, *M*A*S*H* — 172
Antiwar Anthem: Norman Whitfield and Barrett Strong, "War" — 173
Different Paths, Same Destination: Denise Levertov, "Making Peace"; Brian Turner, "The Hurt Locker" — 174
Deserving Better: John Prine, "Sam Stone" — 175
War Hawk: Francis Ford Coppola and Edmund North, *Patton* — 176

18 DYSTOPIAN LANDSCAPES — 179

Women and Unwomen: Margaret Atwood, *The Handmaid's Tale* — 179
Feed the Hungry, but Just Some of Them: Suzanne Collins, *The Hunger Games* — 181

A Second Chance: James Cameron and William Wisher,
    Terminator 2: Judgment Day   182
Opposite Land: George Orwell, *Nineteen Eighty-Four*   183
Your True Calling: Veronica Roth, *Divergent*   184

Hooray, Success!   187
Notes   189
Further Reading, Listening, Viewing, and Exploration   191
Bibliography   199
Index   213
About the Author   219

INTRODUCTION

Back in middle school and through most of my time in high school, I didn't read much. In fact, I often pretended to read the books my teachers assigned to our class. I'd dog-ear the pages and bend up the cover, like that book was going home and back with me on the bus, but it was really sitting in my desk, unread. I'd go so far as to place an oversized bookmark in its pages, hoping to fool my teachers. Then I'd show up to class, listen to the discussion about the story, and even add insights of my own, often putting myself in the main character's shoes.

I actually passed a lot of English classes that way. I was absolutely wrong and only cheating myself. It wasn't that I couldn't read. I just wasn't interested in the books I was given at school. I spent a lot of my free time reading the sports section of the newspaper, watching TV, going to the movies, and memorizing the lyrics to songs I liked. I was actually infatuated with the idea of how writers created stories, but somehow, that infatuation didn't transfer to books.

One day, I had just arrived at English class and was telling a friend all about this great movie I had seen the night before. It was one of the James Bond 007 films. My English teacher overheard heard me and said, "Paul, I'd like to see you in the back of the classroom for a moment."

I figured that I was in trouble. This was English class, and I was busy discussing a movie, not a book. To my surprise, the teacher reached up to a shelf where she kept a classroom library. She handed me a book from the James Bond series by Ian Fleming. Then she said, "That movie you like so much is actually based on this book. And I think the book is even better."

Well, that was the first book I remember reading cover to cover. And it basically started me on the road to becoming an English teacher and an author.

Now about *this* book.

I envisioned its concept and wrote it because it's the type of book I would have wanted to read when I was in school. A book that discusses music, TV, movies, and even superheroes in the same breath as novels, plays, and poems. Why the emphasis on opening lines? Because writers of every genre have one goal in common: to capture the audience's attention with their very first words. And we'd all prefer to be instantly engaged, whether we're reading, watching, or listening.

So I hope you enjoy this book and share it with every preteen, teen, and adult you know who loves the spoken word but may not be a bookworm—the less-than-enthusiastic who is simply waiting for the right book to come along.

ONE

SETTING, MOOD, AND TONE

No matter the genre, every artistic work establishes a mood and a tone, often through a description of the setting, where the action occurs. It's just like when you naturally smile, frown, or look annoyed, others quickly are clued into your mood. The voices and actions of the narrators and characters in a work also play a huge part in signaling the author's intended feeling to the audience. Let's see how that happens.

DARK AND STORMY

OK, we'll start with something completely nonthreatening and fun, and who could fit that bill better than Charles M. Schulz's bookish beagle named Snoopy, a beloved character from the comic strip *Peanuts* (1952–2000) with some very distinctive ties to literature. You see, Snoopy is a writer; one of his many personalities is "World Famous Author." His favorite place to write is sitting on the roof of his doghouse, tapping away at the keys of a typewriter. (And yes, I do believe that Snoopy will one day move on to using a computer keyboard, perhaps even a wireless one.)

Snoopy's go-to opening line as a writer is, "It was a dark and stormy night." Kudos to Schulz for providing us with such a riveting opening, especially because it's almost all we ever see of the cartoon canine's stories. The line provides us with instant setting and tone. After all, it is "dark" and "stormy" outside, and our imaginations are certainly ready to fill in the blanks as to whatever might happen on such a "night." Nothing too scary please. This is *Peanuts* with Charlie Brown and Lucy Van Pelt, not the start of a teen horror flick.

From where did the line "It was a dark and stormy night" originate? Snoopy first typed it in 1965, but three years earlier, author Madeleine L'Engle used it to begin her famed young adult fantasy book *A Wrinkle in Time* (1962). Her narrator, Mrs. Whatsit, begins, "It was a dark and stormy night. In her attic bedroom Margaret Murry, wrapped in an old patchwork quilt, sat on the foot of her bed and watched the trees tossing in the frenzied lashing of the wind."

Nearly a century and a half earlier, English author Edward Bulwar-Lytton wrote the novel *Paul Clifford* (1830). Its rather long and winding opening line: "It was a dark and stormy night; the rain fell in torrents—except at occasional intervals, when it was checked by a violent gust of wind which swept up the streets (for it is in London that our scene lies), rattling along the housetops, and fiercely agitating the scanty flame of the lamps that struggled against the darkness."

Over the succeeding decades, the opening "It was a dark and stormy night," despite its spot-on description of a time and place, was often criticized by reviewers, especially when many novice writers used it to begin their work. It was called "purple prose," meaning something overly ornate in its use of language that takes undue attention away from the story.

Interestingly, the English Department at San José State University in California celebrates the line by holding an annual writing contest in which participants use the phrase to write the best worst sentence. And of course, Schulz was happy to have Snoopy, a fledgling novelist of the first degree, comically use the cliché as his standard opening, no matter what he was writing about.

Our bookish beagle is also a fan of Russian author Leo Tolstoy, reading his masterpiece *War and Peace* at a rate of one word per day. Just so you know, it's an exceedingly long book—587,287 words to be exact. At that pace, it would take Snoopy, who turns 75 in 2025, more than 1,600 years (human, not dog years) to finish. So don't complain about the length of any reading assignment your teacher ever gives you.

> Go ahead. Take a try at completing the opening line "It was a dark and stormy night." What would your next sentence be to keep the appropriate imagery moving forward?

A TALKING RAVEN

Now that you're getting your literary legs beneath you, let's look at another well-known opening that brilliantly establishes setting and tone. On this occasion, however, the writer goes much deeper into detail, not only giving us time, place, and mood, but also transferring those feelings to the protagonist (that's a fancy way of saying main character), who in this case is our narrator. It's all brilliantly done in just a pair of sentences.

The author is Boston-native Edgar Allan Poe (1809–1849), and his narrative poem is "The Raven" (1845). You may already be familiar with its famed opening lines:

> Once upon a midnight dreary, while I pondered, weak and weary,
> Over many a quaint and curious volume of forgotten lore—
> While I nodded, nearly napping, suddenly there came a tapping,
> As of some one gently rapping, rapping at my chamber door.

You can hear the alliteration grabbing the reader's attention with its silky string of *p*'s, *w*'s, *q/c*'s, *n*'s, and *p*'s again, all sounding off in rapid succession.

So it's a "dreary midnight," and the "weak and weary" narrator seems to be alone, reading an old book and on the verge of falling asleep, when there's suddenly a rapping at his chamber door. We're definitely set up for something ominous to happen, and Poe doesn't disappoint us.

The narrator's visitor is a supernatural raven who can speak. No, the raven doesn't say, "Caw." Rather, it speaks English and can say but one word: a resolute "Nevermore"—the answer to whether the narrator will reunite with his lost love, Lenore.

The poem is often celebrated at Halloween because of its dark feel. It has been made into several sci-fi and horror movies and parodied many times, including by *The Simpsons* in their "Treehouse of Horror" episode. Troublemaking Bart Simpson plays the raven, only Bart's version of the supernatural bird doesn't say, "Nevermore." Instead, it utters one of his popularized catchphrases, "Eat my shorts."

The popularity of Poe's poem is the reason that Baltimore's NFL team is called the Ravens. You see, Edgar Allan Poe died in Baltimore and is buried there. His gravesite has become an important tourist attraction. What's the best time to visit a spooky mystery writer's grave to pay homage to his literary talents? Most likely at the stroke of midnight while holding a lit candle. It just seems appropriate.

ANOTHER STARRY NIGHT

While many, including *The Simpsons*, have parodied "The Raven," songwriters often draw inspiration for their lyrics from classic works of either art or history. Singer/songwriter Don McLean did both with the painting *The Starry Night* (1889) by Dutch artist Vincent Van Gogh. The painting shows a seemingly electrified night sky filled with swirling, starlike images, as the horizon is about to turn from darkness to dawn. He painted the scene from his room in an asylum, where he was receiving care for a variety of ongoing mental health challenges after self-mutilating his left ear.

With just a handful of words, McLean, in his song "Vincent" (1971), beautifully pens an opening that reflects both the painting and Van Gogh's turbulent life, establishing essential tone and mood:

> Starry, starry night.
> Paint your pallet blue and grey,
> Look out on a summer's day,
> With eyes that know the darkness in my soul.

McLean's use of personification gives us the instant impression of the sky as a living, breathing entity, perhaps even guiding Van Gogh's hand. It's a sky that perfectly portrays both the beauty in the world and the overwhelming storm raging inside Van Gogh, who died of a self-inflicted gunshot wound approximately two years after painting *The Starry Night*.

Later in the lyrics, McLean speaks directly to the memory of the departed artist, as if the spirit of Van Gogh could somehow find comfort in his forthcoming words:

> But I could have told you, Vincent,
> This world was never meant for one
> As beautiful as you.

The song is a magnificent mix of art, history, and passion, with an opening that instantly vaults the listener onto the perfect plain for the beautiful yet disturbing journey that lies ahead.

> *What color would you say best reflects your personality? Would it ever evolve into a different color over the course of a day, perhaps to reflect your changing mood—say from morning to afternoon or afternoon to evening?*

TWO

IDENTITY

Writers want to instantly connect with their audience. Penning the perfect opening lines sometimes equates to making a spot-on introduction, the same way you might introduce yourself to someone you've just met. For the writer, it's about presenting an immediately interesting character or a distinctive voice to establish an identity. The characters who open a literary or lyrical work often come to us as stick figures or bare-boned skeletons. And as that work moves forward, they are fleshed out with each passing word, until we feel as if we know them.

WOMAN POWERED

Let's begin with a trio of recent pop songs written by some extremely talented singer/songwriters who all made their first impressions on audiences as teens. In each case, these lyricists quickly create an identity through their narrative.

In "Blank Space" (2014), Taylor Swift satirically reintroduces herself to an audience who has been relentlessly bombarded by news and social media stories about the singer/songwriter's love life, labeling her a serial dater of other high-profile stars. As an expert storyteller, Swift uses this to her advantage by crafting a voice that perfectly mirrors such an image. Thus "Blank Space," referring to an opening on a romantic or social calendar, begins with three lines that are partly an introduction and partly a polished pickup line:

> Nice to meet you, where you been?
> I could show you incredible things
> Magic, madness, heaven, sin

The flirtatious narrator wastes no time in getting to the main point. She's looking for a new romantic relationship, and she's totally in charge of the possibility of making that happen.

Of course, thanks to Swift's immense fame, even within the song, she never has to give herself a name. There is no, "Hi, I'm Taylor." That's because, singing as herself, we're supposed to already know her. And she masterfully checks the identity box, filling that nameless void, with the later lyric, "And I know you heard about me."

Then there's the wonderfully tongue-in-cheek line about Swift's supposedly limited worldview as a self-engrossed popstar. Instead of the traditional "read you like a book," she mocks her own image by penning, "I can read you like a magazine." The song is a stunning example of assuming an identity that the media has created, only with the artist playing that role explicitly on her own terms.

Billie Eilish and Finneas O'Connell, homeschooled siblings who began their songwriting journey by studying with their mother, Maggie Baird, who taught a songwriting class in Southern California, wrote "What Was I Made For?" for the 2023 film *Barbie*. The title poses a very appropriate question as Barbie, a life-size doll come to life, undertakes a personal quest, leading her from a pink-hued Barbie Land, where nothing ever changes or goes wrong, to the uncertainty of the real world in order to discover her true identity.

The song opens with the narrative voice, representing Barbie questioning the very core of her existence:

> I used to float, now I just fall down
> I used to know, but I'm not sure now

That leads the protagonist to the undeniable question from which she can no longer sidestep in pink plastic heels: "What was I made for?"

One important theme in *Barbie* is that real women have often felt intimidated and pressured to live up to the unrealistic physical expectations established by the Barbie doll. The songwriters brilliantly capture this sentiment, casting it back onto Barbie herself, with the later lines

> I was an ideal
> Looked so alive, turns out, I'm not real

Filipino American songwriter Olivia Rodrigo, daughter of a schoolteacher and a family counselor, also took on the idea of women being compared to unrealistic body standards in "Jealousy, Jealousy" (2021), only this time, we hear it from the perspective of a teenage voice. Rodrigo, who overcame being born half-deaf in her left ear, introduces us to a voice of female frustration:

> I kinda wanna throw my phone across the room
> 'Cause all I see are girls too good to be true
> With paper-white teeth and perfect bodies

That commonly shared angst among preteens and teens is vital to hear and perfectly presented in the forthcoming lines:

> I know their beauty is not my lack
> But it feels like that weight is on my back

Later we get those much-needed *warning* lines that should make us stop and think, providing self-reflection and possibly cluing us in to what our friends in similar situations might be feeling

> Com-comparison is killing me slowly . . .
> I'm so sick of myself
> I'd rather be, rather be
> Anyone, anyone else.

Perhaps "Jealousy, Jealousy" is a terrific combination of a teen writer, who has also benefitted from hearing her parents speak on such matters, with her eyes wide open.

From popstars to lauded poets, the theme of women being compared to unrealistic physical standards is written about with great depth and passion. Poet and civil rights activist Maya Angelou (1928–2014), however, takes a different tack by introducing us to an uberconfident narrator who totally uproots the notion of a feminine ideal based on body dimensions in "Phenomenal Woman" (1978). Angelou's poem opens with the lines

> Pretty women wonder where my secret lies.
> I'm not cute or built to suit a fashion model's size

The narrator immediately establishes an identity of a societal outsider because she doesn't buy into the norms of others. However, the narrator's annoyance comes not with society but with women who want to understand the foundation of her internal strength and believe her truthful answers to somehow be "telling lies." These strengths that propel her forward in life include the "reach of my arms," "span of my hips," "stride of my step," and finally an element of internal tenacity with the "curl of my lips."

This autobiographical tone by an author who during her lifetime held such diverse jobs as fry cook, sex worker, nightclub performer, news correspondent, director, and producer of plays and films lends an immense weight to Angelou's words. Angelou concludes,

> Phenomenal Woman,
> That's me,

A powerful self-assertion that rings so true.

> *Have you ever felt pressure to live up to the expectations of the so-called perfect body type? Do you believe that such artistic expressions as the ones we've just encountered can help people to better examine and discuss what they're feeling?*

WHAT'S IN A NAME—OR NOT?

Do you know the meaning of your own name? Its roots or origin? Many parents choose a name for their children because of its specific meaning. Correspondingly, writers often give their characters names to inspire a specific response from the audience.

No discussion of establishing an immediate identity, especially through a name, in just a handful of words can be complete without examining what is arguably the most recognizable opening line in all of literature: the line that begins Herman Melville's iconic novel *Moby-Dick* (1851), which bears the double title *The Whale*.

"Call me Ishmael." It's an introduction of the first degree.

The character's instruction to the reader feels rather formal and serious. After all, he isn't asking to be called Bob or Bobby. We're also left to wonder if this is the character's actual name, that he's not asking us to use *Ishmael* as an alias of some sort, perhaps shielding his true identity. That's a lot to ponder from a single line, mirroring Melville's incredible talent as an artist.

Ishmael is a biblical name from the Book of Genesis. He was, in part, an outcast left to wander the desert. The name translates from the original Hebrew as "The Lord will hear." It's an important association (to readers who might either know or look up the meaning), making us feel that the character's words could have far-reaching relevance, as we listen to Ishmael begin his story.

The narration continues, "Some years ago—never mind how long precisely—having little or no money in my purse, and nothing particular to interest me on shore, I thought I would sail about a little and see the watery part of the world."

Our character quickly winds up aboard a whaling ship as a lowly crewmember, committed to a three-year journey. The ship is commanded by Captain Ahab, a fanatical man driven by revenge to harpoon and kill the great white whale Moby Dick. Why? On a previous encounter, the whale bit off one of Ahab's legs. The captain now wears a prosthetic peg leg, ironically made of whalebone. The story rises and swells on a tide of emotions, an epic journey of man versus nature and man versus himself—all launched via an unforgettable opening line.

HAVE A CHOCOLATE?

Now let's consider two different openings to basically the same story. One is a film, and the other is the novel on which that film is based. One opening immediately offers up the character's first and last name as an introduction to the audience, while the other does not. The pair of openings and character in question is Forrest Gump from the film (1994), written by screenwriter Eric Roth, and the novel (1986), authored by Winston Groom, which both share the title *Forrest Gump*.

Forrest is an occupational name, a woodsman. But it also suggests a closeness to the land and an earthy feel. Appropriately, the character is rather humble concerning his many achievements and close associations with multiple important historical events.

In the film's opening, a feather floats down, perhaps from the heavens, eventually landing beside our protagonist, portrayed by actor Tom Hanks, who is seated on a bench at a Savanah, Georgia, bus stop. Forrest places the feather inside a small suitcase, securing it between the pages of the children's book *Curious George* by author H. A. Ray. Is that because Eric Roth, who won an Academy Award for his screenplay, wants to clue us in to the character's childlike nature? Or is it foreshadowing in the story, which will be told through a series of flashbacks, that the main character will eventually be caring for a child of his own?

Before any dialogue, there is visual emphasis placed on both the mud-encrusted Nikes on our character's feet and the box of assorted chocolates in his hand. A bus arrives and then leaves. But Forrest doesn't get on it. Does the protagonist have a deeper purpose for being here?

A Black woman in a nurse's outfit sits down beside him, leading our character to introduce himself. "Hello. My name is Forrest—Forrest Gump. You want a chocolate?" he asks, opening the box and holding it in front of her.

She declines with a simple shake of her head, before Forrest adds, "Momma always said, 'Life is like a box of chocolates. You never know what you're gonna get.'"

Then Forrest looks at her thick-soled, white nursing shoes and comments that they must be very comfortable. The woman answers, "My feet hurt."

In response, Forrest immediately observes, "Momma always says there's an awful lot you could tell by a person's shoes. Where they're going. Where they've been."

It's a brilliantly conceived opening, as we're about to learn of the places, events, triumphs, and disappointments experienced by Forrest after already glimpsing what's on *his* feet.

Now here's a different look at an opening for the same character: Groom's novel begins with Forrest narrating his story: "Let me say this: bein a idiot is no box of chocolates. . . . Now they says folks sposed to be kind to the afflicted, but let me tell you—it ain't always that way."

The purposeful spelling errors in the text are a visual means through which the author reinforces the character's claim that he is in some way "afflicted," with an IQ approaching only 70. The literary opening provides Forrest with a self-deprecating edge to him without alluding to his first name until the opening chapter's fourth paragraph. This leaves "idiot" being our only means of recognition toward him.

Forrest, though, assures us that he's a lot smarter than most people believe at first glance, providing the reader with an insight into the character and soon-to-be unfolding events. It's a superb device conceived by Groom to forge an early bond between Forrest and the audience.

By the way, Groom's novel contains the line "Stupid is as stupid looks." For the film, Roth revised it to read, "Stupid is as stupid does."

> So which of the two openings do you prefer? Consider the differences in genre. The screenwriter has visuals to show us, including a human representation of Forrest. Meanwhile, the author relies more on descriptions and our imagination, with each reader envisioning Forrest in their mind a little differently.

CAN YOU SEE ME?

Here's a completely different point of view by the author Ralph Ellison concerning the introduction to his protagonist/narrator's identity. I suppose you can call the voice of Ellison's novel *Invisible Man* (1952) the "anti-Ishmael" or the "anti–Forrest Gump." That's because throughout the course of the entire story, Ellison chooses for his main character to remain nameless.

The unnamed Black man informs the reader, "I am an invisible man. No, I am not a spook like those who haunted Edgar Allan Poe; nor am I one of your Hollywood-movie ectoplasms. I am a man of substance, of flesh and bone, fiber and liquids—and I might even be said to possess a mind. I am invisible, understand, simply because people refuse to see me." By refusing to give him a name, the writer sets up a scenario where his character is an Everyman representing all people of color, at a moment in history when racial prejudice is unrestrained and often not prosecuted by the authorities.

The narrator resides in an underground room lit by hundreds of bright lights powered by electricity he has stolen from the city. It seems only fitting that a city that seemingly denies his existence freely provides the power for the narrator to see himself. Hence, the city is both blind to his presence and the theft.

In 1983, three decades after its debut, Ralph Ellison spoke about the impact of *Invisible Man* and why the work crossed so many social barriers: "Literature is integrated. And I'm not just talking about color, race. I'm talking about the power of literature to make us recognize again and again the wholeness of the human experience."[1]

> *Think about how you might interact with others if you had no name or if you existed within a society that refused to see you. How would your life and attitudes toward the world around you be different?*

NOBODY IS SOMEBODY

Poet Emily Dickinson (1830–1866) had only a handful of her poems published during her lifetime. It wasn't until after her death that her younger sister found a cache of approximately 1,800 of her elder sibling's writings. In "I'm Nobody! Who Are You?" (1891), the still relatively unknown poet introduces herself:

I'm Nobody! Who are you?
Are you—Nobody—too?
Then there's a pair of us!
Don't tell! They'd advertise—you know!

Considering the playfulness of her self-evaluation, perhaps Emily Dickinson might have been someone fairly immune to the pressures, memes, and even bullying of today's social media. What do you think?

THREE

THE HUMAN CONDITION

Listen to almost any passionate conversation between two or more people, whether it's at home or school; on the street, playground, or athletic field; or in the media or the workplace. The topic of discussion will most likely center on the human condition. That includes our needs, desires, fears, hopes, dreams, sense of right and wrong, happiness, sadness, and continual striving to make both our own lives and the lives of our loved ones better.

Now examine all your favorite poems, plays, films, TV shows, songs, and speeches. You know, the ones that keep running through your head without much prompting. The ones you more or less have committed to memory. Isn't the human condition at the very heart of their focus and appeal, too?

WHY SHAKESPEARE?

One of the many reasons we still read the plays and poems of William Shakespeare (1564–1616) more than four centuries after his death is that the Bard (a title reserved for a much revered poet) was an absolute master at presenting the human condition in all its glory and flaws. During his lifetime, Shakespeare penned some 38 plays (comedies, tragedies, histories, and romances) and more than 150 sonnets—poems comprised of fourteen lines each.

Shakespeare also had a magnificent gift for capturing and holding an audience's attention from the outset, a significant reason his works are so widely read and cherished. By engaging his audience at the start, his works become difficult to put down.

Have you ever felt intimidated by the idea of reading Shakespeare? Know that you're not alone. After all, he does write in early modern

English. But that's only one generation of language removed from the English we speak today. It's probably the same way your parents or grandparents feel whenever they see a teen-oriented TV show or hear a song that uses current slang. So hang in there! I'm confident that you'll be able to piece together the meaning.

> Note: As we explore longer works, including the plays of Shakespeare, we'll widen our perspective a bit to include the opening lines of important scenes and characters who may not be the first to speak. It seems only correct considering the length of these literary works, and the many starts, stops, and pauses authors often provide for their audience.

HAMLET'S DILEMMA

The play *The Tragedy of Hamlet, Prince of Denmark* (c. 1599–1601) opens with the line "Who's there?" It's an intriguing statement because the sentinels standing guard over the castle are about to see what they believe is the ghost of their recently departed king, the father of Prince Hamlet, as Shakespeare immediately brings us to the question of life after death, a major concern of the human condition. Also, there's nothing like the thought of seeing a ghost, a spirit unable to find its rest, to immediately grab the audience's attention.

We don't actually meet Hamlet until the second scene, where he speaks to us in an aside, a device wherein the character uses a "quiet" voice that only the audience can hear, excluding the other characters. In the presence of both King Claudius, formerly his uncle and now his stepfather, and his mother Queen Gertrude, Hamlet describes the new king to us as a "little more than kin and less than kind." What does that mean?

Well, Hamlet hates the fact that his uncle has married his mother, making him twice his kin, or "more than kin"—his uncle *and* stepfather. The "less than kind" part? Hamlet believes that King Claudius murdered his father for the throne. The makings of a dysfunctional family for sure.

Later in the play, Shakespeare again provides the audience direct insight into Prince Hamlet during his soliloquy (a character speaking their thoughts aloud, often with no other actors on the stage). Shakespeare's opening lines of Hamlet's soliloquy throw a perfect strike into the heart of darkness, capturing the human condition at the height of personal doubt, debating whether it is better to live with unbearable injustice or simply die, perhaps in an effort to set that injustice straight.

"To be or not to be—that is the question," ponders Prince Hamlet, who is suffering from severe depression.

> Whether 'tis nobler in the mind to suffer
> The slings and arrows of outrageous fortune,
> Or to take arms against a sea of troubles
> And by opposing, end them.

In plain language: Should Hamlet simply suck it up and accept all the dishonesty going on around him, or is suicide the better option?

With this speech, Shakespeare opens a door for us into Hamlet's soul, giving the audience the opportunity to fully embrace him at his most conflicted and vulnerable point in life—solidifying Shakespeare as a true master of depicting the human condition.

SONGS OF SOCIAL CHANGE

The next several centuries didn't lighten the immense weight of individual and societal struggles nor the daily question of life and death surrounding us all. The 1960s and 1970s were marked by social turmoil, especially for those living in such cities as Chicago, Detroit, Memphis, New York, Los Angeles, and Philadelphia. Overcrowded conditions were spiked by poverty, crime, racism, and a military draft to supply US soldiers for the conflict in Vietnam—with it all sparking protests.

As a reflection of this era in history, singer/songwriter Marvin Gaye penned an anthem of recognition and responsibility in "What's Going On" (1971).

The song begins with a universal statement of grieving:

> Mother, mother
> There's too many of you crying

It's a powerful sentiment that breaks all social boundaries with the unwavering love of a parent for their child. And that opening line binds the audience to the song, even if the upcoming scenarios don't include every listener.

Gaye's focus next shifts to all the people whose lives were cut too short, particularly people of color like himself:

> Brother, brother, brother
> There's far too many of you dying

The writer then pleads for respect from the authorities who dismiss the beliefs of those seeking change, labeling them troublemakers:

> Picket lines and picket signs
> Don't punish us with brutality

And finally, Gaye warns those uncomfortable with the appearance of a younger generation not to ignore their voice:

> Oh, but who are they to judge us
> Simply 'cause our hair is long?

This song was born out of a particular moment in time, which has unfortunately been repeated several times since. A song of love and the frustration at ... what's going on—all brought together by a unifying opening line.

Rapper Jay-Z, whose real name is Shawn Carter, a native of the Marcy Houses (Projects) in Brooklyn, released "Some How Some Way" (2009), an ode to rising above many of the same difficult circumstances detailed by Marvin Gaye decades earlier. He begins,

> Please believe that
> Some how some way
> We gotta make it up out of the hood some day

He is passionately asking his audience not to give up hope and to stay focused on finding a path ahead, with the key word being *we* to connect to the larger audience.

Jay-Z details the ways people have risen above all the traps and deep holes challenging neighborhoods can present for the people who live there. Then he turns to personal experience and how he was part of the problem, recounting the days in which he sold drugs in his neighborhood to make money:

> I'm from the dirt, I planted my seed on unfertile land . . .
> And still I grew

The lyrics end with a tribute to author Betty Smith's novel *A Tree Grows in Brooklyn* (1943), in which the protagonist, young Francie Nolan, lifts herself from an ultrachallenging Brooklyn neighborhood through education by reading a book a day from the public library:

> Look man a tree grows in Brooklyn.

The line is a natural symbol of strength and success.

> *Do you believe that songs like these can inspire people toward their goals? Can a record of what's actually going on in many of our neighborhoods and cities help to bring about positive change, even if it's just a first step?*

WARNING SIGNS

Opposing tribes have been squabbling since the beginning of civilization. Mistrust, paranoia, envy, and fear have unfortunately plagued the human condition, often stoking our darkest elements and either leading us to war or pushing us to the brink of it.

Author and cartoonist Theodore Seuss Geisel (1904–1991), better known as Dr. Seuss, is remembered for his classic children's tales *The Cat in the Hat*, *Green Eggs and Ham*, *Horton Hears a Who*, and *How the Grinch Stole Christmas!* But in 1984, Dr. Seuss released *The Butter Battle Book*, a sobering, cautionary tale about the dangers of nuclear war.

The story starts with a youngster being educated about the world in which he lives by his grandfather: "On the last day of summer, ten hours before fall, my grandfather took me out to the wall." It takes Geisel just a handful of words to establish a foreboding scenario with the images "last day," "fall," and "wall" setting the stage for what's to come.

The youngster is told that the wall separating the Yooks (his family's tribe) and the Zooks (the opposing tribe) has grown much higher over the years. So high, in fact, that the tribes can no longer look each other in the eye. It seems every Zook eats their bread with the buttered side facing down, while the Yooks eat their bread with the buttered side facing up. Their differences simply can't be resolved.

The ensuing conflict starts with sticks and then slingshots, before escalating to guns and explosives. Finally, the Yooks perfect the Bitsy Big-Boy Boomeroo (with an emphasis on *BOOM!*), a small pellet that can blow up the Zooks' half of the world. Naturally, the Zooks invent one equally as damaging. In the closing scene, there's a standoff at the wall, with each side threatening to destroy the other and the entire world. So the opening line's subtle imagery, unfortunately, plays out in the unfolding plot.

The Butter Battle Book may not be what you expect from Dr. Seuss, but it's a powerful statement about the human condition and how our collective flaws could one day conceivably end it.

MOB MENTALITY

Shirley Jackson starts her short story "The Lottery" (1948), about a small town of three hundred, located somewhere in America, turning out for their yearly celebration—a shared community event of sorts: "The morning of June 27th was clear and sunny, with the fresh warmth of a full-summer day; the flowers were blossoming profusely and the grass was richly green. The people of the village began to gather in the square, between the post office and the bank, around ten o'clock."

Could it be a parade? A town picnic? Wouldn't that fit this idyllic opening to a story?

The children have already finished their school year, but instead of being enthused about the oncoming summer, they seemed rather restrained: "the feeling of liberty sat uneasily on most of them." And their talk still centers around school, their teacher, "books and reprimands." The environment begins to feel somewhat controlling and harsh, as the kids help to gather stones.

We learn that the event is called the lottery, only the grand prize may not be what you're expecting. The winner gets to be stoned to death by the rest of the community, a human sacrifice to ensure a good harvest. "Lottery in June, corn be heavy soon" is a local proverb.

YOU CAN DO IT TOO

Can people who live average lives create great literature? The answer is undoubtedly yes. Shirley Jackson wrote "The Lottery" in basically one sitting, after putting her young daughter in her playpen and the frozen vegetables she had just purchased at a supermarket into the refrigerator.

"The Lottery" first appeared in *The New Yorker* magazine and resulted in lots of hate mail and complaints from readers about the story's content.[1] It made even more of an impact because the story was published on June 26, 1948, just one day before the fictional events supposedly take place, making it feel like this could be happening somewhere right now.

A month after "The Lottery" debuted, Shirley Jackson, in an interview with the *San Francisco Chronicle*, commented, "I hoped, by setting a particularly brutal ancient rite in the present and in my own village, to shock the story's readers with a graphic dramatization of the pointless violence and general inhumanity in their own lives."

Remember how the flowers and grass were so lush in the very first line? There are rumors that other towns are stopping their lottery. But here, a mob mentality of purging their town of bad omens still prevails, feeding superstitious fears of being unable to control the natural world around them.

Jackson's second line describing a calm and collective celebration is a perfect example of how basically good people can abandon reasonable thought and even commit murder because the larger group as a whole condones it.

Yikes!

A NEED TO COMMUNICATE

German-born Anne Frank was given an autograph book, which she promptly turned into a diary, for her thirteenth birthday. Her very first entry in those pages expresses a deep desire to communicate her thoughts and feelings, even if she was going to be the only one to ever read them: "12th June 1942: I hope I will be able to confide everything to you, as I have never been able to confide in anyone, and I hope you will be a great source of comfort and support."

Shortly thereafter, Anne and her family, who were Jewish, were forced into hiding to avoid being sent to a Nazi concentration camp. For two years, the Franks hid in a concealed room behind a bookcase in the Amsterdam attic of her father's business, whose employees were willing to risk their own lives by concealing them. But nothing stopped Anne, who wanted desperately to become a writer, from making diary entries:

> 5th April 1944: If I don't have the talent to write books or newspaper articles, I can always write for myself. But I want to achieve more than that. . . . I want to be useful or bring enjoyment to all people, even those I've never met. I want to go on living even after my death. . . . When I write I can shake off all my cares. My sorrow disappears, my spirits are revived.

The Frank family was discovered by the Nazis in August 1944 and imprisoned. Anne died at the age of fifteen in the Bergen-Belsen concentration camp. Her father, the lone member of the Frank family to survive the camps, published her diaries in 1947, after the conclusion of World War II. With the publication of *The Diary of a Young Girl*, Anne's dream of being a writer came true, and her words live on after her death.

> *Have you ever kept a private diary or journal? Did anyone ever read it without permission? If so, did you feel proud or violated? Do you think Anne would have wanted her personal diary shared with the world?*

THE PLIGHT OF ADDICTION

Sadly, another aspect of the human condition is addiction, especially to drugs and alcohol. Many artists have tackled the subject head-on, either relating stories of personal experience or by recounting what they've seen happen to others.

Drugs and alcohol have been a contributing factor in the deaths of many artists and writers: Prince, Michael Jackson, Kurt Cobain, Edgar Allan Poe, Jimi Hendrix, Janis Joplin, Dylan Thomas, Charles Dickens, Ernest Hemingway, Robert Louis Stevenson, Jack Kerouac, and F. Scott Fitzgerald, to name a few.

Singer/songwriter Pink (Alecia Moore) penned "Sober" (2008), which begins,

> I don't wanna be the girl who laughs the loudest
> Or the girl who never wants to be alone

It's a pinpoint view of the devices we often use in order to sidestep our issues, fears, and unhappiness:

> I'm safe up high
> Nothing can touch me

Then comes the overwhelming question of how to change your life for the better:

> But how do I feel this good sober?

Pink acknowledges that there are no easy answers, only the hard work of bettering your life.

Poet Selena Odom's "My Master" (2010) gets directly to the matter of who is really in charge of a relationship between someone and their addiction:

> I have a master of an evil kind.
> He totally controls my body, soul and mind.

Odom eventually entered into recovery after writing these opening lines during the depths of her addiction.

British singer Amy Winehouse, who had a long history of substance abuse, passed away in 2011 at age twenty-seven, at the height of her career. Several years earlier, Winehouse had ironically released the song "Rehab" (2006), which opens,

> They tried to make me go to rehab, but I said, "No, no, no."

It was once believed that artists could open their minds and be more creative while being high or intoxicated. Writer Stephen King, who has given us such classic horror stories as *Pet Sematary* (1983), *Carrie* (1974), *Cujo* (1981), *The Shining* (1977), and *Christine* (1983), has been in recovery for more than three decades, is quick to dispel that mistaken notion. "The idea that the creative endeavor and mind-altering substances are entwined is one of the great pop-intellectual myths of our time. Substance abusing writers are just substance abusers," said King.[2]

Canadian-born singer/songwriter Neil Young reflects on the misery of heroin addiction in "The Needle and the Damage Done." The song opens with the lines, "I caught you knocking at my cellar door. I love you, baby, can I have some more?"

The need for the next "fix" can be enslaving, even causing addicts to sell their own blood for drug money:

I know that some of you don't understand
Milk-blood to keep from running out

Nothing in Young's song romanticizes the use of hard drugs. There isn't even a mention of a brief euphoria. The omission is purposeful because the end result of heroin use is so devastating.

Young concludes by associating the addict's journey with the most appropriate image imaginable:

I've seen the needle and the damage done
A little part of it in everyone
But every junkie's like a settin' sun.

Fade out.

FOUR

SELF-DETERMINATION

Literature can be incredibly empowering to an audience. Many artists also find their inspiration in the self-determination of people with a passionate desire to improve both themselves and the world that surrounds them. In this chapter, we encounter several forms of expression—from plays to poems to songs—that mirror those feelings, all with indelible opening lines, including an immeasurably important open letter penned by civil rights activist Martin Luther King Jr. at the height of the battle for equal rights in the United States.

MAKING YOUR OWN WAY

The musical *Hamilton*, with book and lyrics by Lin-Manuel Miranda, debuted onstage in 2015. It took Miranda, a native New Yorker of Puerto Rican heritage, seven years to write this awe-inspiring slice of American history retold in a modern format, through the lens of rhythm and blues, hip-hop, soul, pop, and traditional showtunes—the ultimate mixed bag of musical genres. It is based on the 2004 biography *Alexander Hamilton* by Ron Chernow.

Miranda, who originally starred in the title role himself, immediately reaches for a connection to the audience through the opening line, posed by a member of the onstage cast. It is a vital and well-conceived question that begs an answer, thus giving the audience an important stake in the rapidly unfolding story to come. That initial question also presents a glimpse into Hamilton's personal mythology, giving us insight into the protagonist whom we are about to meet.

A cast member asks the audience,

> How does a bastard, orphan, son of a whore and a
> Scotsman, dropped in the middle of a forgotten
> Spot in the Caribbean by providence, impoverished, in squalor
> Grow up to be a hero and a scholar?

The answer most likely going through the audience's mind is, "Self-determination." The protagonist, an absolute underdog as described, must possess incredible resolve.

Later in the opening, those thoughts are confirmed in the lyrics by other members of the cast:

> by working a lot harder
> By being a lot smarter, by being a self-starter

As the opening's tension builds, a cast member asks of the still-shadowed protagonist,

> What's your name, man?

Stepping into the spotlight, the protagonist answers,

> My name is Alexander Hamilton.
> And there's a million things I haven't done
> But just you wait, just you wait.

It's an amazing opening sequence that propels the musical forward, creating a bond between the title character and the audience. And Miranda's decision to employ color-blind casting, often using actors of color to represent historical figures who were not of color, opens a door even wider.

"Our cast looks like America looks now, and that's certainly intentional," noted Miranda. "It's a way of pulling you into the story and allowing you to leave whatever cultural baggage you have about the founding fathers at the door."[1]

CHANGE BY EXAMPLE

Michael Jackson, the "King of Pop," had a megahit with a song of self-determination and social change, titled "Man in the Mirror" (1987), cowritten with Glen Ballard and Siedah Garrett. The song begins,

> I'm gonna make a change
> Gonna make a difference

The emphasis is squarely on the shoulders of the narrator and no one else.

The song is a statement about the stark reality of closing our eyes to people's suffering, believing that others will take the lead in offering help:

> I see the kids in the street
> With not enough to eat
> Who am I to be blind
> Pretending not to see their needs?

The chorus circles back to the narrator as a vital cog in solving such problems—the same way we can all be empowered to help:

> I'm starting with the man in the mirror
> I'm asking him to change his ways

It's a message of personal responsibility concerning society at large:

> And no message could've been any clearer
> If you wanna make the world a better place
> Take a look at yourself and then make a change

Two years earlier, Michael Jackson and singer/songwriter Lionel Richie penned "We Are the World" (1985), a song aimed at raising funds and awareness to aid the people of Ethiopia suffering from famine.

The opening lines are direct and to the point, describing a moment in history that must be acted on:

> There comes a time when we heed a certain call
> When the world must come together as one

The description goes on to pull no punches in detailing the harsh landscape and desperately needed help:

> There are people dying
> Oh, and it's time to lend a hand to life
> The greatest gift of all

The inclusiveness and weight of the narrative voice grows exponentially with the introduction of the song's chorus, performed in harmony by a multitude of famous musicians:

> We are the world, we are the children
> We are the ones who make a brighter day
> So let's start giving.

The notion of self-determination and its importance also arises in the chorus:

> Oh, there's a choice we're making
> We're saving our own lives

More than fifty recording artists, collectively known as USA for Africa, lent their voices and talents to the recording and accompanying music video, which raised more than $10 million in humanitarian aid for those in need.

> *Was there ever a time in your life when you said to yourself, "Someone needs to do something to help, and that someone is me"? What moved you to such a decision?*

FROM BEHIND BARS

Dr. Martin Luther King Jr., recognized for his nonviolent protests, was a man of great self-determination who preached that concept to others. His followers turned out for protest marches and boycotts across the country to stand up to racial injustices. King firmly believed that people, refusing to accept anything less than total equality, could spur political and social change through their combined voices.

A recognized public speaker, King was also a brilliant writer. In April 1963, he penned "Letter from a Birmingham Jail" to those in opposition of his cause. Along with Reverend Ralph Abernathy, Martin Luther King Jr. was arrested for leading a peaceful protest, challenging segregation in Birmingham's public accommodations, such as city busses.

During his eight-day stay in jail, King wrote his public letter, which begins, "While confined here in the Birmingham city jail, I came across your recent statement calling my present activities 'unwise and untimely.'" It is a strategic start on the part of King to pit logic against illogic. Of course, those who would deny people their rights to equality normally believe that any attempt to change the status quo would arrive at the wrong time.

The Alabama-based critics of King, from Atlanta, Georgia, called him an "outsider." An *outsider* in his own country?

King's response: "I am cognizant of the interrelatedness of all communities and states." Then King addresses the crux of the matter, reminding those who oppose basic freedoms of their own intentional shortsightedness: "You deplore the demonstrations taking place in Birmingham. But your statement, I am sorry to say, fails to express a similar concern for the conditions that brought about the demonstrations."

The letter concludes, "Let us all hope that the dark clouds of racial prejudice will soon pass away and the deep fog of misunderstanding will be lifted from our fear drenched communities. And in some not too distant tomorrow the radiant stars of love and brotherhood will shine over our great nation with all their scintillating beauty."

It is appropriately signed, "Yours for the cause of Peace and Brotherhood, Martin Luther King, Jr."

> *In which ways might a handwritten letter, even in today's electronic-based society, be more powerful than a text or an email?*

THE TRAP OF HATRED

Author and poet Wendell Berry, who hails from Henry County, Kentucky, was awarded the National Humanities Medal by President Barack Obama. His poem "Enemies" (1994) preaches the self-determination and discipline not to become like those who would do you harm. In essence, it promotes participating in a peaceable disagreement and resolving problems without violence. The poem begins,

> If you are not to become a monster,
> you must care what they think.

The poet/narrator instantly involves the reader by associating the thought of becoming a "monster" with "you," not them. And will you "care" enough to at least consider their point of view and what motivates their belief?

Berry then asks a question that has been posed over the ages in many ways, concerning intense conflict between people or nations residing on opposing sides of a passionate issue:

> how will you not hate them,
> and so become a monster
> of the opposite kind?

The poem's core suggestion is simply "forgiveness," without relying on the threat of war to bring about peace. That's because violence gives you but one option, while a peaceful response may provide the opportunity to open new doors of discussion.

DOUBLE STANDARD

Do you believe that people are treated differently in our society because of their gender? If so, has that ever made you uncomfortable, annoyed, or even envious? Perhaps you might have wished that you could trade places with someone of a different gender for a while, just to experience being seen or treated differently. Let's look at a pair of pop songs that interestingly explore those thoughts.

Songwriters Gwen Stefani and Tom Dumont coauthored the wonderfully satirical "I'm Just a Girl" (1997), which begins,

> Take this pink ribbon off my eyes
> I'm exposed and it's no big surprise

The lyrics instantly challenge society's limited view of what it means to be female:

> Oh, I'm just a girl, all pretty and petite
> So don't let me have any rights

And just so you understand the true point of the piece and don't take the lyrics simply at face value, the cowriters send a blunt message to the listening audience:

> Oh, am I making myself clear?

In other words, are you getting the sarcasm?

Though the narrator is a supremely strong woman, the uphill climb against society's perceived gender roles remains somewhat daunting:

> I'm just a girl in the world
> That's all you'll let me be.

> *Does it make a difference to you, positively or negatively, that the song was cowritten by a male?*

Beyoncé Knowles-Carter, a native of Houston, Texas, makes an equally powerful statement about gender with her song "If I Were a Boy" (2008):

If I were a boy, even for just a day

Knowles-Carter makes the point that if her wish came true, she could "throw on" whatever clothes she wanted, "drink beer with the guys, and chase after girls" with no condemnations or consequences from society for her actions. All because she'd be a boy and not a girl—the very definition of a double standard.

If Beyoncé were a boy, she believes that she'd "know how it feels to love a girl" and actually "listen to her," not taking her for "granted." Ironically, the narrative voice assures us, "I'd swear I'd be a better man."

The writing is so spot-on that the audience probably believes that she would be better at being a man than a large percentage of the male population. The song is a marvelously revealing statement about the societal roles assigned and tolerated by gender.

FIVE

TIME AND SPACE

TO BOLDLY GO

Actor William Shatner played Captain James Tiberius Kirk on the original TV series *Star Trek* (1966–1969), created by Gene Roddenberry. The episodes, almost without exception, begin with Captain Kirk speaking to the audience during the show's title sequences: "Space: the final frontier. These are the voyages of the starship *Enterprise*." Both the writing and Shatner's dramatic delivery of the opening lines establish an instantaneous connection with the audience, securing their complete attention.

The introduction continues with Shatner articulating, "It's five-year mission: to explore strange new worlds, to seek out new life and new civilizations." Then the final line is enunciated with a sense of rising energy and purpose: "To boldly go where no man has gone before." The *boldness* emphasized here resonates as much today as it did more than a half-century ago, with modern-day space pioneers currently searching galaxies beyond our own for new life forms and answers that may secure Earth's ultimate survival.

The full introduction, which consists of thirty-seven words packed into just a pair of sentences, is itself a lesson on how to write economically with no wasted words. Bravo!

Nearly two decades later, the series was revived as *Star Trek: The Next Generation* (1987–1994). So what about that classic introduction?

This time around, actor Patrick Stewart, who portrays Captain Jean-Luc Picard, reads during the title sequences. However, the word *man* was removed from the original copy, and the final line was revised to read "to boldly go where *no one* has gone before," thus making it gender neutral.

That change was also partly in recognition of the women astronauts and cosmonauts (the Russian equivalent) who had gone into space during the early 1980s, including American Sally Ride aboard the space shuttle *Challenger* in 1983.

FROM SCIENCE FICTION TO REALITY

Of course, when *Star Trek* first appeared on the air in 1966, astronauts had not yet landed on the moon. That didn't happen until July 21, 1969, when the lunar module of *Apollo 11* settled onto the moon's powdery surface in a section designated as the Sea of Tranquility.

Astronaut Neil Armstrong, the voice of the first words spoken on the moon, transmitted the good news of the module's safe landing back to NASA's mission control on Earth: "Houston, Tranquility base here. The Eagle has landed." Though quite accurate, that statement was rather technical and ho-hum.

But for Armstrong's first steps on the moon, his accompanying message wouldn't disappoint. As he set foot on the lunar surface, the first human to do so, he said, "That's one small step for man, one giant leap for mankind."

His perfect choice of words had both weight and gravity (pun intended) to them. The astronaut had maintained for some time that his speech was spontaneous and just came to him at the moment. But he once confirmed that he and his wife, Janet, had previously discussed what he would say.

Even an astronaut walking on the moon can feel like a joyful child. And Armstrong acted just that way while looking out at the distant Earth. "It suddenly struck me that that tiny pea, pretty and blue, was the Earth. I put up my thumb and shut one eye, and my thumb blotted out the planet Earth. I didn't feel like a giant. I felt very, very small," said a humbled Armstrong.[1]

MAY THE FORCE BE WITH YOU

One of the great opening lines in film isn't spoken. Instead, it's printed, to be read by the audience. George Lucas's *Star Wars* (1977) begins, "A long time ago in a galaxy far, far away." The blue words appear on-screen against a black background accompanied by a soundtrack of complete silence. It's not until that line disappears that the screen is filled with the immensity of a billion stars (a typical galaxy contains 10 billion), and what should be the silent vacuum of space is shattered by the opening strains of composer John Williams's dynamic music. Of course, there's more reading to come with the iconic upward rolling scroll of golden text, which explains the backstory of the epic civil war between the evil Galactic Empire and the heroic Rebel Alliance.

So which character actually delivers the first spoken line in the initial *Star Wars* film, subtitled *Episode IV—A New Hope*? Why, it's the golden droid C-3PO. Frazzled by a huge on-ship explosion, the compulsively worrisome humanoid robot, voiced by actor Anthony Daniels, says, "Did you hear that? They shut down the main reactor. We'll be destroyed for sure." To which his more focused electronic counterpart, R2-D2, responds with a series of high-pitched whistles.

More important than the opening lines of specific characters is the musical score that accompanies their first moments on-screen. Before Darth Vader ever speaks, we hear the dark and foreboding "The Empire," coupled with his mechanical breathing from behind that masked helmet. That lets us know that his intentions are purely evil. In sharp contrast, Luke Skywalker's accompanying music, "Luke's Theme," is melodic and uplifting, signaling him as a character to be trusted and embraced. The music representing these two characters is so different that we would never guess that they are actually father and son (hopefully I didn't spoil that for anyone).

Next time you watch any installment of the *Star Wars* franchise, listen for the music that accompanies each character's appearance on-screen. It should tell you something about them, even before they speak.

> **SPACE PARODY?**
>
> In the film *Spaceballs* (1987), writer/director Mel Brooks parodied George Lucas's iconic opening line to *Star Wars*: "Once upon a time warp . . . in a galaxy very, very, very, very, far away," penned Brooks. In fact, Brooks's upward scrolling graphics comically conclude with, "If you can read this, you don't need glasses."

AI GONE WRONG

The film *2001: A Space Odyssey* (1968) by Stanley Kubrick and Arthur C. Clarke is also a novel (1968) by Arthur C. Clarke. The twin stories deal with human evolution, artificial intelligence, and extraterrestrial life visiting Earth.

The unlikely star of the proceedings, especially in the film, is a manmade on-ship computer named HAL, who first speaks by introducing himself to the crew: "Good afternoon, gentlemen. I am a HAL 9000 computer. I became operational at the H.A.L. plant in Urbana, Illinois, on the twelfth of January 1999."

The character both thrilled and panicked audiences. You see, HAL, represented by a singular glowing red eye with a yellow, sunlike pupil, controls all the functions to keep the five astronauts, three in suspended animation and two conscious, alive as the ship travels through space, far from Earth.

The AI seems safe and polite enough, but HAL begins to develop human emotions, including fear. And after malfunctioning at a task, proving the computer isn't perfect, HAL worries that he will be turned off and therefore die. The renegade computer becomes willing to kill in order not to be killed.

"I think you know what the problem is just as well as I do," HAL informs Commander Dave Bowman, the lone remaining astronaut with the ability to stop the AI. "I know that you and Frank [now dead] were planning to disconnect me. And that's something I cannot allow to happen."

That's quite a change in tone and intent from HAL's opening line, wouldn't you agree? That's what makes the computer's revolt even scarier—how quickly it develops a dangerously self-serving personality.

Considering today's debate over AI—from film stars being replaced by virtual actors to students using it to write their papers and teachers even using it to grade them—Kubrick and Clarke were ahead of their time in penning this story.

> *Just imagine if your AI at home, Siri, Alexa, or Google Assistant, wanted to harm you. How might you be able to reason with or outthink such an opponent?*

HITCHHIKING

A comedic, sci-fi novel? Don't laugh at the idea! In author Douglas Adams's *The Hitchhiker's Guide to the Galaxy* (1979), based on a radio series previously penned by Adams, the Earth and its inhabitants aren't really respected much throughout the cosmos. The novel's opening lines establish that fact quite well:

> Far out in the uncharted backwaters of the unfashionable end of the Western Spiral arm of the Galaxy lies a small unregarded yellow sun. Orbiting this at a distance of roughly ninety-eight million miles is an utterly insignificant little blue-green planet whose ape-descended life forms are so amazingly primitive that they still think digital watches are a pretty neat idea.

You'd think our world would have at least a little galactic swag, but not so. To prove it, the Earth is blown up by a race of unpleasant, businesslike aliens called the Vogons. What did Earthlings do to them? Nothing really. They just needed to make room for a hyperspace bypass. Why? I suppose interstellar traffic can be horrifying at rush hour.

Adams's cast of characters includes Earth's lone survivor, an Englishman named Arthur Dent, and Marvin the Paranoid Android, who suffers from bouts of extreme depression and boredom.

More space comedy? The characters eventually discover that Earth was really a supercomputer designed by another supercomputer named Deep Thought, which was originally built to solve "The Ultimate Question of Life, the Universe, and Everything."

Hold on tight. The answer might be as simple as 42 (not kidding).

The perfectly penned opening line by Adams sets the tone that we're not as important as we think and the universe certainly doesn't revolve around us!

BETTER READ OR ELSE

Damon Knight's short story "To Serve Man" (1950) is the perfect cautionary tale for nonreaders. The plot has aliens called the Kanamit visiting Earth, offering to help us in many ways through their advanced knowledge. No one is saying that you should judge a book by its cover. But Knight's opening lines describing these otherworldly beings should give the audience plenty of pause in trusting them: "The Kanamit were not very pretty, it's true. They looked something like pigs and something like people, and that is not an attractive combination."

The piglike humanoids bring our civilization cheap, unlimited power and an endless supply of food; a device that suppresses explosions, rendering armies nearly useless; and new drugs that can prolong human life. It all seems like a wonderful new friendship with these altruistic aliens who want nothing in return. But not everyone totally trusts them.

The story's narrator and a friend eventually get their hands on a Kanamit dictionary and then one of their books, *How to Serve Man*. "I've read the first paragraph of that book. . . . It's a cookbook," the friend tells the narrator in sheer terror. Hey, is this cosmic payback for humans inventing bacon?

Like I've been telling you, opening lines are incredibly revealing, no matter from which galaxy a book comes. That's why you should always read the book yourself and not trust someone else's notes. You might wind up on the wrong side of the buffet table!

Knight's story was also made into an episode of *The Twilight Zone*, "To Serve Man" (1962), with the teleplay written by series creator

Rod Serling, who changed the aliens from pigs to nine-foot-tall domed-headed creatures with massive strength.

Serling ends the episode with some superb writing, with man going from "dust to dessert" and from holding dominion over a planet to an "ingredient in someone's soup."

"It's tonight's bill of fare from *The Twilight Zone*," concludes Serling in a perfect deadpan (again, a purposeful pun).

WARRING WORLDS

English author H. G. Wells published the science-fiction novel *The War of the Worlds* in 1897, and the masterfully written book hasn't been out of print since. The story, seemingly light-years ahead of its time, inspired generations of writers and scientists, including Dr. Robert Goddard, who ultimately invented the liquid-fueled rocket.

The novel begins, "No one would have believed in the last years of the nineteenth century that this world was being watched keenly and closely by intelligences greater than man's and yet as mortal as his own; that as men busied themselves about their various concerns they were scrutinized and studied."

The Martians have been watching us and waiting. And with their own natural resources dwindling, they arrive on Earth to colonize us by force using a chemical weapon in the form of a poisonous black smoke. Interestingly, Wells compares the Martians to the many earthly empires that have colonized weaker civilizations and countries. In that respect, the narrator views the alien invaders as simply carrying out a long tradition of the strong conquering the weak: "And before we judge of them too harshly we must remember what ruthless and utter destruction our own species has wrought. . . . Are we such apostles of mercy as to complain if the Martians warred in the same spirit?"

Don't worry too much. Eventually, humankind gets its revenge on the invaders via Mother Nature. That's as far as I'll go in terms of a spoiler, but remember, the novel's very first sentence informs us that these aliens, though possessing a greater intelligence than Earthlings, are just as "mortal."

PUBLIC PANIC

Many plays and films have been based on Wells's work, including the 2005 movie *War of the Worlds*, starring Tom Cruise. But none have quite made the same impact as a 1938 radio broadcast on Halloween Eve, in which scores of listeners believed Earth was being invaded by Mars.

An announcer opened, "Ladies and gentlemen, we interrupt our program of dance music to bring you a special bulletin." It's absolute genius on the part of Wells, making it sound like an actual alert and not part of the broadcast.

The voice went on to explain that gaseous explosions emanating from Mars were moving toward Earth with tremendous velocity. Throughout the regularly scheduled show, there continued to be interruptions from correspondents in the field interviewing fictitious professionals from such real institutions as Princeton about the ongoing alien invasion.

"This is the most terrifying thing I have ever witnessed," reported an on-scene correspondent. "Someone's crawling out of the hollow top (of a spaceship). Someone or something."

Though at the time there was an outcry from Congress concerning the public fear the broadcast had caused, it wasn't until 1992—after several more modern on-air media hoaxes—that the Federal Communications Commission (FCC) instituted a rule against such broadcasts, unless there were adequate disclaimers stating that the material wasn't real.

> Would you believe a newscast you heard stating that aliens had just landed on Earth? How might you go about checking it out?

SIX

THE ROAD, STREETS, AND OTHER TRAVELS

Perhaps you really enjoy taking road trips, experiencing new and exciting places with your family and friends. You play multiple rounds of car bingo, I Spy, or the license plate game to make the miles go even faster. Please, if you play punch buggy, don't hit anyone in the arm too hard when you spot a Volkswagen Beetle, even if it's a yellow one.

Artists in various genres have also embraced the concept of the road in their work, drawing great inspiration from its symbolism and common connection to us all. The road often stands for freedom and the linking together of people from different parts of the country. In this chapter, you'll journey alongside these artists and several of their iconic characters. So buckle up your seatbelts, and get ready. And, no, you may not call shotgun.

NOTHING TO HIDE

One of the great works of literature is John Steinbeck's *The Grapes of Wrath* (1939). It focuses on the journey of the Joad family, farmers traveling from Oklahoma, which has been ravaged by dust storms, to what they hope will be a land of plenty—California. Not only had dust storms crippled the livelihood of many prairie and high-plains farmers after several years of intense drought, but the Great Depression (1929–1939) also severely injured the economy.

The story begins with Tom Joad hitchhiking back home. The first words Tom speaks are to a trucker who is walking to his rig after making a stop for food: "Could ya give me a lift, mister?"

The trucker reluctantly obliges and during some conversation on the road learns that Tom hasn't seen his family in some time. The driver is curious about Tom, asking questions concerning his absence.

Tom responds, "I'll tell you anything. I ain't hidin' nothing.... The name's Joad. Tom Joad."

After a while, the trucker notices Tom's new clothes and shoes and pieces together that he has just been released from prison. Tom tells us that he was convicted and served four years for a homicide in self-defense.

It's an amazing scene in which the nosy trucker goes to great lengths in trying to read Tom, who is already an absolute open book. It's the author's way of letting the audience know that Tom will always be truthful with us and that we can trust him.

Why is that so vital to the novel?

The Joad family eventually reunites and takes their beat-up truck on the road via Route 66 to California. Along the way they encounter all kinds of dishonesty with large farm owners trying to cheat them and other migrant workers living in tent cities out of an honest day's pay picking fruit. There are also threats of violence from the local authorities, who are paid off by the big farm owners, against any migrant worker who dares to speak out against the corrupt system.

A Joad family friend, preacher Jim Casy, is senselessly killed by their oppressors, after standing up for himself and the rights of others. Tom, who witnesses the attack, clubs and kills Casy's murderer with a pickax. Now an outlaw, Tom leaves his family to protect them, vowing to help all people in need.

Before hitting the road for good, Tom tells his mother, "Wherever you can look—wherever there's a fight, so hungry people can eat, I'll be there. Wherever there's a cop beatin' up a guy, I'll be there."

Tom becomes a modern-day Robin Hood or avenger, pledging to help the poor and abused, which is why it was so important for us to view Tom Joad as totally honest in Steinbeck's roadside introduction of him.

THE BOSS VOICES TOM

New Jersey native Bruce Springsteen (a.k.a. the Boss) was so moved by Steinbeck's character that he penned a song "The Ghost of Tom

Joad" (1995) to reflect an economic downturn in the mid-1990s, resulting in fewer jobs and increased homelessness.

The song opens in great doubt, with a procession of homeless people heading to a place of which they are not exactly sure:

> Men walking along the railroad tracks
> Going someplace, there's no going back

The narrator sees immense lines at the shelters, with people sleeping in their cars or cardboard boxes and bathing in the city aqueduct:

> Well the highway is alive tonight
> But nobody's kidding nobody about where it goes

The highway is alive with people driving or walking—people without homes or jobs—most likely heading for a heartbreaking destination, where eventually they'll do what they have to do to survive.

Then Springsteen paraphrases Tom's farewell speech to his mom:

> Wherever somebody's struggling to be free
> Look in their eyes, Ma, and you'll see me

Some subjects, no matter the era, are so worthy of discussion that they come around again and again—unfortunately.

NOBODY STREET

Mexican-born poet Octavio Paz, awarded the 1990 Nobel Prize in literature, is a master of rhythm, perspective, and imagery. In "The Street" (1963), he travels along a desolate path, passionately believing that someone else must be heading for a similar destination as himself:

> Here is a long and silent street.
> I walk in blackness and I stumble and fall
> and rise, and I walk blind

The opening lines deftly set us in motion, following the speaker, almost blindly ourselves.

The speaker can hear and feel someone walking behind, slowing whenever he slows down and gathering speed whenever he does, as well. But when he turns around to look everything is "dark and doorless," with "nobody" in sight.

After turning seemingly endless street corners leading nowhere, the speaker finally notices someone walking up ahead. Like him, that person stumbles and rises in a mirror image of himself, instantly bringing us back to the poem's opening.

When that unknown person turns around to face the speaker, definitively seeing him, he says, "nobody." It's an extraordinary scenario from a writer who, because of his piercing blue eyes, at first glance wasn't believed to be Mexican or completely accepted as such by those with whom he grew up.

> Have you ever felt alienated or isolated by others, even if you felt a strong bond toward them yourself?

YOU DECIDE

Poet Robert Frost presents us with quite the quandary in "The Road Not Taken" (1916). The poem opens with the narrator needing to make a difficult choice:

> Two roads diverged in a yellow wood,
> And sorry I could not travel both
> And be one traveler

It's a problem with which everyone can associate, coming to a fork in the road and needing to make a decision of which path to choose. Only this decision doesn't really seem to be about finding a shortcut home but rather which direction to choose in life. The narrator knows that he may never be exactly here again, so the choice could be incredibly meaningful.

Finally, after long internal debate, the narrator chooses the road less traveled, appearing to be less worn, but then he quickly contradicts the thought by telling us that both roads appear more or less equally unworn by foot traffic.

The dilemma of the opening line, to a point, has been sweetly solved by the narrator. Because both roads are for all intents and purposes judged to be *the same*, he can figuratively travel them both. A major copout?

Suddenly, the narrator projects himself into the future, looking back at this decision:

> I shall be telling this with a sigh
> Somewhere ages and ages hence

A *sigh*, not a celebration?
The poem concludes,

> Two roads diverged in a wood, and I—
> I took the one less traveled by,
> And that has made all the difference.

Take notice of the hesitant pause between *I* and *I*, as if trying to gather some confidence to convince himself. Is the narrator trying too hard not to be wrong in his choice? Is this an early stage of FOMO (fear of missing out)? Or is this poem simply an enigma for you to project onto your own life at your next major crossroads?

> *Look back at a positive or negative choice you have made in your life. Give yourself honest feedback about what swayed your decision at the time. If you suddenly had the chance to choose differently, would you?*

CHANGING COURSE

English singer/songwriter Adele, cowriting with Greg Kurstin, penned a rather personal piece that touched on Frost's notion of the "road less traveled," her song "I Drink Wine" (2021). Adele, whose estranged father suffered from severe problems with alcohol, had just started down the road to becoming sober herself.

Her song opens with the question,

> How can one become so bounded
> By choices that somebody else makes?

The line fully opens the door to self-reflection, exploring reasons we live our lives the way we do and how much the actions of others might somehow influence our own choices.

She asks,

> Why am I seeking approval
> From people I don't even know?

I suppose that even superstars have their doubts and need to be reassured.

The singer makes it perfectly clear that though she's touched on the same road as her father—comforted by the company of alcohol—she's now changing course. With a nod to Robert Frost in the rearview mirror, Adele affirms,

> Sometimes the road less traveled
> Is a road best left behind

THEY'RE YOUR FOOTSTEPS

Walt Whitman (1819–1892) is one of the world's most recognized and widely read poets. His work often focuses on his core belief of the basic goodness in both humankind and nature.

In contrast to Frost, the narrator of Whitman's free-verse poem "Song of the Open Road" (1856) proclaims that his life will not be dictated by the confines of a particular path or road but by his own choosing.

The piece begins,

> Afoot and light-hearted I take to the open road,
> Healthy, free, the world before me,
> The long brown path before me leading wherever I choose.

The narrator does not need luck to succeed in life:

> I myself am good-fortune, . . .
> Strong and content I travel the open road

There is no personal hesitancy for Whitman, no daunting decision on which to dwell, because his road is "open," not confined by set borders. The poet even challenges the road on which he advances:

> O highway I travel, do you say to me, "Do not leave me?" Do you say,
> "Venture not—if you leave me you are lost?"

Whitman, however, is having none of that and proclaims his total independence:

> From this hour I ordain myself loosed of limits and imaginary lines.

It's a perfect reflection of the key images in the poem's opening lines: "light-hearted," "free," and "I choose." To this day, Walt Whitman's poetic spirit is undoubtedly still roaming free in the hearts of his readers.

> *Are you more like Frost's narrator, wondering where the road will take you, or Whitman's poetic voice, making your own way and unconcerned about veering off the established road?*

ON THE WIND, YOU SAY?

Robert Zimmerman, who was born in Duluth, Minnesota, adopted the alias Bob Dylan in recognition of his favorite poet, Dylan Thomas (1914–1953). As a songwriter, Bob Dylan was dubbed "The Voice of a Generation," with his lyrical expressions becoming anthems of peace and positive change, starting in the 1960s and continuing into the new millennium. In 2016, Dylan was awarded the Nobel Prize in literature for his immense body of songwriting.

One of those songs, "Blowin' in the Wind" (1962), which starts the listener down a road of reflection and introspection, poses some very poignant questions. The piece begins,

> How many roads must a man walk down
> Before you call him a man?

It's a question with both broad societal and personal implications.

Dylan asks a question to which no one can give an absolute answer. That's part of what makes it so appealing to the audience. It's all about your opinion and no one else's. Listeners now have an active stake in the song, with more opinions to follow.

In considering acts of war and destruction, Dylan inquires,

> Yes, and how many times must the cannonballs fly
> Before they're forever banned?

These are questions that have touched on our collective consciousness for centuries, yet we can't seem to solve them. That's why it's perfectly suitable for Dylan to assert in the chorus,

> The answer, my friend, is blowin' in the wind.
> The answer is blowin' in the wind

We can all hear and feel the answer on the wind, only it's too elusive to grasp. Still the solutions are tapping each one of us on the shoulder, waiting to be acted on.

Each time the chorus comes around, it reminds the listener that the answers to these prolific questions are really not so far away. They're swirling all around us, waiting to be corralled and acted on. In fact, the answers are "blowin' in the wind."

SEVEN

SPORTS

Sports can be an amazing vehicle, providing us with a sense of individual achievement as well as an opportunity to bond with others, be they our teammates or even our rivals. Perhaps it's a sport, such as basketball, track and field, swimming, field hockey, martial arts, lacrosse, pickleball, or maybe even quidditch, that specifically aligns *your* body and mind as one. No matter your personal preference of sport, all athletes share a common purpose: to push themselves toward excellence.

Writers have long been moved and inspired by sports and their participants, whether it's the Olympic Games or weekend warriors doing battle on a Saturday afternoon at their local park. And maybe as you read these writers' opening lines, you'll see yourself in the situations and athletic events they so deftly describe. Even if you don't consider yourself an athlete, the passion of these pieces may just move you to shelve your electronic devices for a few hours and participate in a sport yourself.

ATTENTION GETTING

ABC's *Wide World of Sports* (1961–1997) was a weekly show that made a huge impact on viewers by highlighting varied and often unique sports, from Mexican cliff diving to hurling to badminton to logger games. With such ever-changing content, something about the show needed to be constant. That consistency came from the incredible intro, written by Stanley Ralph Ross and voiced by legendary sportscaster Jim McKay.

"Spanning the globe to bring you the constant variety of sports," begins McKay in a crisp tone. The screen fills with the image of youngsters celebrating victory in the Little League World Series alongside McKay's next line: "The thrill of victory." Suddenly, a lone ski jumper, Vinko Bogataj of Slovenia, is flying down an immense snow-covered ramp nearly 172 feet high. (Bogataj became both a semicelebrity and a symbol of bad luck. His injuries? Amazingly, not even a broken bone.) Before he ever takes flight, the jumper crashes, his body contorting wildly and skidding off the side of the ramp, alongside McKay's "And the agony of defeat." McKay's stirring delivery of the text concludes, "This is ABC's *Wide World of Sports!*"

Why is this introduction so devastatingly great? Between the visuals and the audio, there's barely a moment to breathe or reflect, just enough time to react. It's like getting caught up in a whirlwind of words and images that sweeps you away.

LAPOEM JAMES

Some people simply play sports. Others, with remarkable talent, hard work, and desire, become their chosen sport. In many ways, the image, name, and likeness of LeBron James *is* basketball.

LeBron is also a native of Akron, Ohio, a proud city that embraces the achievements of their own. Is it possible to meld a person with both a sport and a city? Poet Sean Thomas Dougherty does just that in his joyful and celebratory poem "Biography of LeBron as Ohio" (2018). The piece opens with a question:

> When is a poem one word?

The answer most likely ringing in the reader's ear, especially after reading the title of the poem, is LeBron.

Thomas begins by comparing the basketball player to the divine greatness of those in other disciplines, especially music:

> Even at 17 he was Baraka
>   on the court, Coltrane gold toned, . . .
>   . . . he was one word like Prince

SPORTS 55

Baraka is an Islamic blessing from God, often bestowed on supremely talented and charismatic individuals. John Coltrane was a jazz saxophonist who could entrance an audience with his golden tones, while Prince, a groundbreaking virtuoso guitarist and electrifying performer, could play many instruments at a high level.

Then Dougherty connects LeBron, who came right out of high school and entered the NBA, to Akron, a hard-working city known as the "Rubber Capital of the World," where car tires had been made for generations:

> hip hop
> blaring from his headphones, all rubber soled
>   & grit as the city which birthed him.

The connection is even easier because "King James" played his first seven NBA seasons for the Cleveland Cavaliers, just forty miles from Akron.

The poet also recognizes the social barriers that LeBron broke with his talent on the court and ability to be a role model in life for others:

> He was every kid, every street . . . he was white
>   & black & brown & migrant kids working farms.

Then LeBron left Ohio, signing with the Miami Heat. There were plenty of hard feelings among the local fans, even shouts at James for his disloyalty. But a few years later, LeBron returned to the Cavaliers, bringing Cleveland its first-ever NBA championship, and reforging a bond with his Ohio-based fans.

Dougherty, trying to get into the head of a basketball god, inquires,

> Does LeBron think of dying?

The answer comes in the form of a magnificent literary image:

> Does the grape think of dying as it withers on the vine by the lake?
>   Or does it dream of the wine it will become?

Through the final lines, LeBron is again the undeniable reflection of where he is from:

> he is a part of this asphalt court we call Ohio, & how we suffer, & how we shine.

Cue the cheering fans in the stands and streets.

Ultimately, the entire piece is a testament and answer to the opening line: "When is a poem one word?" You know the answer. Simply say it in your head.

> *Is there a particular sport that embodies you and your personality? How are you like that sport? How is that sport like you?*

REMEMBER WHEN?

Unlike LeBron James, "Ex-Basketball Player" (1993) by John Updike is a poem about a player whose career didn't pan out past high school. Here's the opening line:

> Pearl Avenue runs past the high-school lot,
> Bends with the trolley tracks, and stops, cut off
> Before it has a chance to go two blocks

Updike is already providing us with an image that suddenly stops short of expectations. Pearl Avenue ends, and the poet brings us to Berth's Garage where our protagonist, Flick Webb, works part-time. We're told "Flick stands tall" among the gas pumps, "their rubber elbows hanging loose and low," a lot like players on the court.

Flick's history? He played for the Wizards, his high school team, and still holds the county scoring record for points. He was absolutely a natural at the game. It seems the "ball loved Flick," and "his hands were like wild birds"—both in the past tense. Yet his name, Flick, most likely a nickname praising his sudden and sharp athletic movements, remains intact. Still Flick relives his glory days every now and then, when, "as a gag," he "dribbles an inner tube" around Berth's Garage.

In the opening line, John Updike provides us with an image that suddenly stops short of expectations. He's talking about Pearl Avenue. But before too long, that image is expertly cast onto the life of our protagonist. Obviously Flick has pride in his accomplishments, but do you consider him to be a heroic or tragic character?

> Why do you believe some people might live in the past, without putting a greater emphasis on their future?

SURF'S UP!

Journalist Susan Orlean penned an incredible article about teen female surfers on the island of Maui in Hawaii, in a small town named Hana. The piece is aptly titled "Life's Swell" (2002). Her work instantly captures the attention and imagination of readers, many of whom are not surfers. That's because Orlean focuses on something to which nearly everyone can relate, using images that are both striking and descriptive to create a mental picture, no matter what your experience at the beach might be: "The Maui surfer girls love each other's hair. It is awesome hair, long and bleached by the sun, and it falls over their shoulders straight, like water, or in squiggles, like seaweed, or in waves." And, of course, their hair is affected by their surfing lifestyle.

Turns out there isn't much to do in Hana except surf, and the author treats that like a precious prize the teens have won: "There is no mall in Hana, no Starbucks, no shoe store, no Hello Kitty store, no movie theater—just trees, bushes, flowers, and gnarly surf that breaks rough at the bottom of the rocky beach."

Surfing has long been viewed as an act of freedom, taming the power of the sea to test your abilities on a fiberglass board, with sharp-toothed waves snapping at your bare heels: "To be a girl surfer is even cooler, wilder, and more modern than being a guy surfer: Surfing has always been such a male sport . . . ; to be a girl surfer is to be all that surfing represents, plus the extra charge of being a girl in a tough guy's domain."

The teens that Orlean interviewed for her story wanted to know something about her life, as well. They were surprised that Orlean came from Ohio, a state not bordered by an ocean, and shocked, that, despite her infatuation with the sport, she had never been on a surfboard in her life.

"What I didn't say was that I'm not sure that at [age] 15 I had . . . the indomitable sense of myself that you seem to need in order to look at this wild water and think, I will glide on top of those waves," noted Susan.

One of the girls made her promise to try surfing one day. "I promised," noted Orlean in the final line of her story.

> Have you ever been a passionate fan of a sport in which you had never participated? If so, would you like to attempt that sport one day?

WIDE SHOULDERS

I suppose we all imagine that being a sports superstar would be a fantastic life. But if you're that talented, there's bound to be immense pressure placed on your shoulders, as well. Can you always succeed? Here's a poem by Ernest Lawrence Thayer (1863–1940) about a famous baseball player stepping up to the plate in one of those pressure-packed moments, with the eyes and expectations of everyone on him. "Casey at the Bat" (1888) was written during an era in which participation trophies didn't exist. Thayer opens,

> The outlook wasn't brilliant for the Mudville nine that day:
> The score stood four to two, with but one inning more to play

This line establishes the name of a team, the score, and the inning of the game. That's pretty impressive, especially because it also rhymes.

Mudville? Is that an early emphasis by the poet that this team needs to be pulled up from the depths of despair? There actually is a town in Massachusetts called Mudville. Residents there claim their town to be the inspiration for the poem, but Thayer had always claimed his setting to be fictitious.

In the poem, we're told that if only Casey could come to bat for Mudville, they'd have a chance. But there are a pair of batters ahead of Casey and already two outs. Amazingly, both batters get base hits, giving Casey a chance for Mudville to be victorious.

The crowd begins to cheer at the top of their lungs. Their unified voices

> pounded on the mountain and recoiled upon the flat,
> For Casey, mighty Casey, was advancing to the bat.

There's some sporting drama for you! And a literary technique called hyperbole at its best. That's an exaggeration that almost certainly couldn't be true; we know that Casey doesn't hit a home run every time at bat or that the voices of the fans actually "pounded" a nearby mountain. But the audience goes along with it anyway because Thayer has our attention, and we *want* to believe:

> Ten thousand eyes were on him as he rubbed his hands with dirt;
> Five thousand tongues applauded when he wiped them on his shirt.

Casey lets the first two pitches go by without ever taking a swing. Both are called strikes by the umpire.

> And now the pitcher holds the ball, and now he lets it go,
> And now the air is shattered by the force of Casey's blow.

Hooray! Casey finally swings!

Only the poet doesn't immediately tell us the result. That's part of Thayer's brilliance as a writer, keeping the audience involved from the first sentence, which perfectly gives all the necessary details, to the last word:

> Oh, somewhere in this favored land the sun is shining bright,
> The band is playing somewhere, and somewhere hearts are light;
> And somewhere men are laughing, and somewhere children shout,
> But there is no joy in Mudville—mighty Casey has struck out.

And if the audience picked up on any negative expectations because of the name *Mudville*, that, too, has been satisfied by Thayer.

> *Was Casey overconfident? Arrogant? Was he possibly nervous? Was he set up for failure? Reading Thayer's poem in full will probably help you to make a better assessment.*

A PRICE TO PAY?

Athletes often get hurt. Unfortunately, sometimes those injuries can be extreme and even life changing. British journalist and rugby player Eva Holland provides a firsthand account as a spectator to such a moment in her story "Why We Play" (2014).

The opening sentence on one level makes us cringe yet on another level invests us in caring about the outcome: "I can still hear the quick crunch of his vertebrae cracking. That's the meddling of hindsight, of course—he was too far away, out in the middle of the night-dark field, and there were too many people around me and around him."

That's a horrific sound, though the speaker is wondering whether it was amplified in her mind because she already knows the end result. And hear the alliteration—*quick, crunch, cracking*. One thing was certain, though: The author understood something was terribly wrong. Over her years in the sport, she'd witnessed plenty of men and women injured in scrums over possession of a rugby ball, but not like this: "In all those other instances the spinal boards had been only precautionary. Everyone knew, this time, that something was different."

Sadly, the player's massive injuries left him paralyzed. The author despises the conciliatory, Band-Aid-like platitudes she would soon hear about the incident, including "He was doing what he loved [playing rugby]."

Some of the author's rugby-playing friends and teammates considered quitting the sport, and she pondered the pros and cons of that notion, as well: "If 'doing what I loved' cost me the use of my legs and my arms, or the full use of my brain, would I say it was worth it? . . . What had the sport given me, and how much was I willing to pay in return?"

Holland undoubtedly has her readers asking the same question of themselves, no matter which sport or activity they are passionate about—a terrific transfer of internal debate from the author to the audience, spurred on by an opening line that makes us feel so much.

FIGHTER, DEFENDER, AND ADVOCATE

Born in Louisville, Kentucky, boxer and activist Muhammad Ali, a three-time Heavyweight World Champion and Olympic gold medalist, was nicknamed "The Greatest" for his seemingly otherworldly athletic ability. But Ali was also a poet, with many around the world, including his former opponents in the ring, knowing his famous tagline, "Float like a butterfly, sting like a bee."

Ali had changed his name from Cassius Clay to embrace the Muslim faith. Then came the draft, which required young men to enter the military and fight in the Vietnam conflict. Ali lost his license to box for several years after he was convicted of refusing induction into the US military on the grounds of religious objection. Eventually, the US Supreme Court overturned Ali's conviction in a unanimous decision. Ali's poem "I Am America" reflects part of his journey. The opening lines are straightforward and unapologetic: "I am America. I am the part you won't recognize. But get used to me." Ali is confronting anyone who may not want to acknowledge his constitutional right to be who he wants to be and share in the fruits of this country. And his detractors at the time were many—people who were angry and didn't understand his beliefs. *How could a boxer not want to fight?*

In subsequent lines, Ali emphasizes, "My name," "My religion," and "My goals." It is a symbolic framing of his journey through both the legal system and the court of public opinion.

Muhammad Ali passed away in 2016 after years of battling Parkinson's disease. At the time of his death, he was one of the best-known, most-respected, and most-loved individuals on the planet. He cared passionately about the rights of the less fortunate and those who might be persecuted for their religious beliefs in all corners of the globe.

One of the champ's favorite self-penned sayings was, "Wars on nations are fought to change maps, but wars on poverty are fought to map change." Ali's words are a reflection of his belief that for too long the needs of poor people have been placed a distant second to the needs of powerful governments.

RIGHT FIELD IS FOR HEROES

Have you ever felt hopelessly unathletic? Perhaps the worst player on a team? If so, Willy Welch's song "Right Field" (1993), performed by Peter, Paul, and Mary, may find a place in your heart: It begins,

> Saturday summers when I was a kid
> We'd run to the schoolyard, here's what we did

They would choose sides for a game; in this case, baseball. The song's narrator calls it a "measure of my self-esteem." Unfortunately, the youngster is always picked last and positioned out in right field, where little ever seems to happen. It's an opening that perfectly presents someone desperately in need of a psychological and social boost—and a line to which many listeners, both male and female, can relate, recalling their childhood insecurities.

The narrator starts to daydream during the game. He doesn't know the inning, score, or how many outs have been made. Suddenly, there's a commotion on the field, and everyone is looking at him, pointing skyward. The ball, almost magically, falls into the narrator's glove. His life and self-perspective have instantly changed immensely for the better. He proclaims,

> Here in right field, it's important you know
> You gotta know how to catch, you gotta know how to throw

We leave our narrator as the new guardian of right field, standing amid the grass "just watching the dandelions grow." Do you think he'll be chosen last again for next Saturday's game?

> *Can you recall a time when you achieved something wonderful playing a sport or a game, even if it was only for a brief moment, and it made you feel ten feet tall?*

NO-NONSENSE CONSCIENCE

Sherman Alexie is a Native American writer from Spokane, Washington. His poem "Victory" (2015) deals with the narrator's guilt after stealing something he really wanted, something his family could not afford:

> When I was twelve, I shoplifted a pair
> Of basketball shoes.

It's the kind of opening sentence that normally steers us away from rooting for the narrator. The author, however, has a different plan, as we witness the sneaker thief pay a steep, self-imposed price for his actions.

You see, once the narrator ties the sneakers onto his feet, he can't hit a shot. Everything out of his hand just "clanked" off the rim. Poor play or his conscience sending a stern message?

In a fit of frustration, the youngster flings those "immoral shoes" into the river. He goes back to playing in his old shoes, which were barely holding together and almost the "same as playing in bare feet." The result is painful "blisters the size of dimes and quarters" on his heels and toes. What an ironic turn of phrase to depict the shoplifter's blisters in terms of money.

Eventually, the youngster confesses to his father, who weeps out of shame. But the lesson is learned. The pair move forward, and the father even manages a laugh while bandaging his son's wounds. By the end of this wonderfully engineered poem, Alexie has counterbalanced his opening line and brought the youngster back into our good graces. Kudos!

> *Do you believe we're more apt to forgive a twelve-year-old for committing a theft than we are an adult? If so, what might be your reasoning?*

PIT STOP 1

Reflecting on What You've Seen and What's to Come, Plus Potential Projects

Here we are, approximately one-third of the way through our journey in discovering and experiencing perfectly penned opening lines and how they affect the audience moving forward. Have you been moved enough by any of the writing to either go online or to your school or local library and experience the entire piece in its original presentation? Because you absolutely can!

Maybe at this point in the proceedings you're ready to tackle the opening line "It was a dark and stormy night," finishing your own version of the well-known opening line. Snoopy would certainly be proud.

Or perhaps you're ready to write a poem or song about your favorite athlete. Maybe rewrite the ending to "Casey at the Bat" and have the once-mighty protagonist not strikeout.

You've also discovered that looking at the work of Shakespeare doesn't have to be confusing or a mystery due to the language. That's good, because you'll encounter his work again later in this book.

So let's get ready to forge ahead and see what other literary masterpieces and perfectly penned opening lines are awaiting us. Perhaps one of your favorite songs, poems, novels, plays, movies, TV shows, or short stories will be coming on the succeeding pages just around the bend.

EIGHT

FREEDOM AND CAPTIVITY, SUPERS AND SLEUTHS

FREEDOM AND CAPTIVITY

Free time, free thoughts, and the freedom to express yourself—those are just a few of the ways in which people celebrate their ability to be individuals in our society. The concept of freedom, along with either the struggle to fully achieve it or the moments when it has seemingly been stripped from our grasp, has moved artists of all genres.

In this chapter, I present the concepts of freedom and captivity, as well as the punishment—deserved or undeserved—that often accompanies imprisonment. We'll also have some fun looking at supers and sleuths, along with their quest of keeping the innocent free and putting wrongdoers behind bars—at least until the next episode, season, or blockbuster movie.

A JURY OF YOUR PEERS?

Reginald Rose's *Twelve Angry Men* (1954) made its appearance first as a TV play and then as a stage production (before becoming an Academy Award–winning film in 1957). It is a courtroom drama focusing on the deliberation of a jury. As you can probably assume by the title, all twelve of the jurors are men, with no women on the panel.

The production begins with a dark stage. As the lights slowly start to come up, we hear the voice of the presiding judge from offstage. The opening sentences instantly grab the audience's attention, cluing us in to the immense gravity of the situation: "Murder in the first-degree ... premeditated homicide ... is the most serious charge tried in our criminal courts."

The jury deliberations are to come. As the lights come up fully, the stage is set as a jury room, with twelve uncomfortable-looking wooden chairs around a large, oblong table, with a clock on the wall to mark the time. Then, the jury files in to take their places.

The opening line is powerful because it basically puts the audience in the role of the jury receiving instructions from the judge. And this isn't just any court case. It's murder in the first degree, premeditated and planned out. So the audience should be intently focused, ready to access and give an opinion on the evidence to come.

It is often mistakenly believed that women could not be jurors during the 1950s. That held true for only a few US states (Mississippi was the last state to approve women jurors, in 1968). The play is set in New York, where women were serving on juries since the late 1930s thanks to the suffragette movement fighting for equal rights. However, women who didn't want to serve could easily get waivers to be dismissed at that time. And Rose, who had been on a real-life jury comprised of twelve men before writing the play, wanted to explore the best and worst qualities of male characteristics and stereotypes. His jurors were depicted as leaders, followers, jokers, bullies, and thinkers who were both analytical and prejudiced in their thoughts.

Who is the accused? We don't really know. But as the jury replays the facts of the case, we start to learn more about the young man on trial. What is his ethnicity? The audience's own racial stereotypes are examined as they try to envision a face in the unfolding story. It's part of the beauty of Rose's writing and conception of this drama. We do know that all the jurors are White and that if the young man is found guilty, he'll face the death penalty.

In many modern productions based on Rose's original story, the jury has a number of women and racially diverse members. The play was made into a 1957 film of the same name, with the screenplay also written by Rose, which won a slew of awards and earned a 100 percent rating on Rotten Tomatoes.

> *If you were ever on trial, would you want a jury like the one in* Twelve Angry Men, *or would you want a jury much more diverse? What do you think diversity might bring to a deliberating jury as they try to interpret the facts?*

CHAINS OF THE MIND

During the last two years of his life, Jamaican singer/songwriter Bob Marley (1945–1981) penned an anthem of freedom titled "Redemption Song" (1980). Its opening details the Caribbean slave trade:

> Old pirates, yes, they rob I
> Sold I to the merchant ships
> Minutes after they took I
> From the bottomless pit

The "bottomless pit" refers to the hold of a ship where abducted human beings were placed like cargo, one on top of the other, in stifling and cramped conditions, often struggling for air to breathe. It is also a horrifying image that mirrors being sent to hell. Great Britain gained control of Jamaica in the mid-seventeenth century and allowed pirates a safe haven to harass the Spanish shipping industry. The island imported approximately two million captured slaves from West Africa to work the sugarcane plantations there.

But Marley has inner strength and sees an ultimate freedom through his faith as a Rastafarian while being tested in his earthly life. The lasting oppression Marely warns about is self-oppression:

> Emancipate yourselves from mental slavery
> None but ourselves can free our minds

The line finds its origins in a 1937 speech given by Marcus Garvey, a Jamaican political activist and the country's first national hero.

"Redemption Song" is a masterpiece of straightforward expression, delivered by a solitary singer accompanied by a lone guitar, bringing even more emphasis to the notion that one person can initiate a revolution of freedom.

BROKEN AND TRANSFORMED

German-born writer Franz Kafka, using fantastical imagery and situations, has penned several short stories in which his protagonists deal with an oppressive loss of freedom and domination by powerful bureaucracies. Two of his very best pieces are "In the Penal Colony" (1919) and *The Metamorphosis* (1915).

"In the Penal Colony" begins with the military execution of a soldier by his own side: "'It's a remarkable piece of apparatus,' ... said the officer to the (visiting) explorer. ... The explorer seemed to have accepted merely of politeness ... the invitation to watch the execution of a soldier." What exactly is the "apparatus?"

It's a nightmarish machine that physically carves the crime into the body of the accused over a twelve-hour period, finally resulting in death. And of course, there is no trial beforehand because the powers that be are never wrong in their accusations. So much for a jury of your peers in Kafka's world. This soldier's crime is not saluting his superior's door once every hour while performing a night watch.

The one saving grace to the horrifically brutal sentence? The apparatus is supposed to give the condemned a glimpse of total understanding of this world and the next during his final hours. Remember, in the opening sentence the officer describes the apparatus as "remarkable," not horrifying. That's an instant indication of the world Kafka has created for us.

Psst. This time something goes wrong with the deadly machine. No more can be said without spoiling the story for those who have not yet read it!

BUG OFF!

Gregor Samsa is the protagonist in Kafka's *The Metamorphosis*. The opening sentences are both powerful and disturbing, riveting the audience to a journey of a man who has seemingly overnight become a hideous, giant bug: "One morning, when Gregor Samsa woke from troubled dreams, he found himself transformed in his bed into a horrible vermin. He lay on his armor-like back, and if he lifted his head a little he could see his brown belly, slightly domed and divided by arches into stiff sections."

Most of his ungrateful family treats Gregor, a traveling salesman and their lone means of financial support, like the ugly creature he has become, keeping him locked in his room. Will this treatment contribute to keeping Gregor, who is extremely conscious of his situation, in his present form? Will the protagonist forget what it's like to be human as he crawls on ceilings and walls, hiding under the sofa whenever somebody from outside enters?

Kafka's portrait of a human who becomes less than human leaves us wondering exactly who is being punished here and why. Did Gregor somehow do this to himself by accepting less than he deserved from everyone in his life? Or is this metamorphosis simply the result of a world that often treats people as vermin?

SEPARATE AND UNEQUAL

Poet Maya Angelou beautifully balances the concepts of freedom and captivity in the piece "Caged Bird" (1983). The opening line tells of a bird with the world spread wide before it—the ideal circumstance of freedom:

> A free bird leaps
> on the back of the wind
> and floats downstream
> till the current ends...
> and dares to claim the sky.

Of course, the writer knows that not all birds, or people, have the same opportunity to choose and explore their own direction. The life of a caged bird?

> But a bird that stalks
> down his narrow cage
> can seldom see through
> his bars of rage...
> so he opens his throat to sing.

The emotions of anger and fear are closely intertwined in human experience, and Angelou makes that connection for us:

> The caged bird sings
> with a fearful trill
> of things unknown

Despite being regularly fed and given shelter, the shackled bird isn't satisfied. There is a great calling of self-determination that is missing in its life. Hence, Angelou assures us that, the caged bird "sings of freedom," yearning for that ideal so beautifully described in her opening line.

> *If you were provided with everything you needed for a comfortable life except for your freedom, would you agree to live that way?*

LIFE ON THE INSIDE

You might be familiar with the film *The Shawshank Redemption* (1994), but the screenplay written by Frank Darabont is actually based on a novella by Stephen King, *Rita Hayworth and Shawshank Redemption* (1982). King's work begins with his narrator, Red, who has spent most of his adult life behind bars and found a calling for himself as the guy who can get you almost anything: "There's a guy like me in every state and federal prison in America, I guess—I'm the guy who can get it for you."

Get exactly what? Contraband—items an inmate shouldn't have in prison, such as "tailor-made cigarettes," a "bag of reefer," a "bottle of brandy" or "anything else within reason." That opening line provides a purpose for Red in his life behind bars, making him feel useful and prideful. And because he's the narrator, we want to trust in him, believe in his viewpoint. It's important for us to know that he's smart—smart enough to sneak things into prison.

Red also introduces us to his coprotagonist, Andy, a newbie at Shawshank Prison in Maine who was convicted of killing his wife and her lover. What does Andy want from Red? A rock hammer, to slowly, over the course of years, dig his way to freedom. That's where Rita Hayworth comes in. She was a famous actress and pinup model during the 1940s, when the story is set. Andy uses her poster to cover the hole he's digging in his cell.

Now let's shift gears and examine an opening line of a later scene from the film, after a scene shift. Andy is sitting alone in the prison's exercise yard, in the shadow of the high wall, when Red joins him. "My wife used to say I'm a hard man to know," Andy confides in Red, and us. "Like a closed book. Complained about it all the time."

Andy believes he drove his wife into the arms of another man, and though he insists that he didn't physically murder them, he feels as if the outcome is *his* fault, that if he could have been more open, his wife would have never begun a relationship with someone else.

An innocent man, paying his own self-imposed sentence. It's an insightful look into someone described as a "closed book," with the audience being taken into his confidence as he secures a bond with Andy.

Red worries about eventually being paroled. His skills of getting people things they want might not translate to the outside because he would have been in competition with the yellow pages (a phonebook for advertisers at that time). Now imagine if Red were released today. Could he really compete against the likes of Google and Amazon? Probably not.

> *If you were stuck behind bars, what might you ask someone like Red to get you from the outside?*

PROPER MANNERS AND PENANCE

The punishment of paying for one's attempted crime has never been more amusing than in the hands of famed writer Langston Hughes, from Joplin, Missouri. His short story "Thank You, M'am" (1991) pits a young boy—a would-be purse snatcher—named Roger against a hurricane of an older woman named Mrs. Luella Bates Washington Jones. The story begins, "She was a large woman with a large purse that had everything in it but hammer and nails. . . . It was about eleven o'clock at night, and she was walking alone, when a boy ran up behind her and tried to snatch her purse."

This opening line perfectly establishes the lopsided battle of wills to come. Simply put, Luella is a mountain of a woman. Why just examine the length of her twenty-nine-letter, ten-syllable proper name. How could she possibly be strong-armed by a Roger?

Luella boots the boy in the behind, then demands that he pick her purse up off the ground, dropped in the botched theft, and hand it to her.

"Now ain't you ashamed of yourself?" demands Luella.

With little choice, and held firmly in Luella's strong grasp, Roger is quite contrite: "I'm very sorry, lady. I'm sorry."

But the lesson isn't over and Luella drags Roger home with her. She admonishes, "You ought to be my son. I would teach you right from wrong.... Are you hungry?"

They arrive at the boardinghouse where she lives, with Luella making Roger wash his face and comb his hair, as she prepares the boy a meal. Roger wants to run now that he's loose, only he doesn't want to damage Luella's opinion of him again, so he remains.

Roger finally confesses why he wanted to steal Luella's purse (I won't ruin it for you). Hughes uses Roger's rather selfish reason and Luella's response to ultimately set the youngster on an honest path, hoping to never disappoint or encounter Mrs. Luella Bates Washington Jones again.

Back to the first line: What did Luella have in that oversized purse? A lot of people smarts and a lot of tough love.

SUPERS AND SLEUTHS

I don't think any of the supers I'm about to discuss could rival Langston Hughes's Mrs. Luella Bates Washington Jones in putting potential criminals on the straight and narrow path. After all, don't most superheroes lock up the same villain several times? I believe Luella's recidivism rate would be much lower than theirs! Still, supers have a clearly defined role in comics, TV, and film: to ensure that good triumphs over evil.

REVISED STEEL

Jerome Siegel and Joe Shuster created Superman, but their *original* opening lines fell completely flat. Why? They first envisioned Superman as an unwitting evildoer under the mind control of a scientist who had forced a drug on him, resulting in incredible strength. It wasn't until Siegel and Shuster turned their creation into the very first superhero in 1938, with a new backstory about being sent to Earth from a dying planet, that audiences began to embrace the character.

The first time we see Superman in costume, he is accompanied by these lines: "Superman! Champion of the oppressed. The physical marvel who had sworn to devote his existence to helping those in need!"

Let's analyze. The authors are playing an interesting game with the audience. Superman is brand new and just being introduced to the public, yet he's billed as "champion of the oppressed," as if he's had a long history of stopping crime. Should we trust Superman? Well, he had "sworn" to help others. And if you can't take the very first superhero at his word, then what's this comic-book world coming to?

We all know that Superman is in love with his *Daily Planet* coworker Lois Lane. What's the first thing that Superman, in the guise of fellow reporter Clark Kent, says to Lois in the pages of a comic book? He hesitantly stutters, "W-what do you say to a—er—date tonight, Lois?"

Very smooth. I suppose that Clark Kent missed the memo from the human resources department about no office romances.

A DARK CRUSADER

Because of the success of Superman, Batman, created by Bob Kane and Bill Finger, appeared a year later in 1939 to become society's second superhero, even though he possessed no otherworldly powers. He did have a darker side, however: looking to avenge the murder of his parents, which he witnessed as a youngster.

The character is described in the opening sentences of his first comic appearance: "The 'Bat-Man,' a mysterious and adventurous figure fighting for righteousness and apprehending the wrongdoer, in his lone battle against the evil forces of society. . . . His identity remains unknown." It's an introduction meant to leave us still somewhat in the dark about the crime fighter.

Let's also note the different types of words and images used to describe the pair: Superman is a "champion" but Batman is "mysterious." That's an odd labeling because we don't know the true identity of either. Batman fights the "forces of evil," while Superman protects the "oppressed." Both supers are part of DC Comics, and the publisher is obviously trying to promote them in different ways to basically the same readership. It's like if Coke and Pepsi were owned by the same company.

OPENING THE DOOR WIDER

Wonder Woman came along in 1941, three years after the start of World War II, as the first female super. Her emergence coincided with women in America assuming jobs traditionally held by men, who were in the armed services fighting the Nazis and Axis Powers overseas.

She is introduced in the comics, "With the beauty of Aphrodite, the wisdom of Athena, the strength of Hercules and the speed of Mercury, this glamorous Amazon Princess flashes vividly across America's horizon from that mysterious Paradise Isle, where women rule supreme." So a female super is described as having great "beauty" and being "glamorous." Funny how the male supers aren't described as handsome or fashionably stylish, even though they're clad in spandex and wear capes.

Wonder Woman's creator was psychologist Dr. William Moulton Marston, who also had a hand in inventing an early version of the polygraph, or lie detector. Interestingly, Wonder Woman's Golden Lasso prevents you from lying whenever you're bound by it.

Though Wonder Woman had lots of immediate fans, she also had many detractors, feeling this powerful female, who didn't need a man in her life to be successful, was sending the wrong message to young girls across America.

WEB SLINGER

Cocreators Stan Lee and Steve Ditko debuted Spider-Man in 1962. The super's first words to the public appear on the cover of Marvel Comics' *Amazing Fantasy*, no. 15. While swinging above a busy city street on a stream of webbing, with a criminal firmly secured in his grasp, Spidey says,

> Though the world may mock Peter Parker, the timid teenager . . .
> . . . It will soon marvel at the awesome might of . . . Spider-Man!

The opening line highlights the duality of the protagonist as both a bullied teen and an emerging super. It's an example of amazingly swift character development.

Writer Stan Lee was a master of using alliteration, which helps the reader remember language. Consider the alliterative power Lee achieved in the opening pair of sentences attributed to Spider-Man: "may mock," "Peter Parker," "timid teenager," "marvel" and "might." Awesome alliteration!

> *If you could become a superhero, which powers would you choose for yourself? What public name might you choose? Would you wear a special costume or outfit? How would your presence make the world a better place in which to live?*

HEY, SHERLOCK

Sleuth finds its roots in the Old Norse word *sloth* for *trail*. Following a trail became known as *sleuthing*. There is even a type of bloodhound called a sleuth hound. By the late nineteenth century, *sleuth* began to refer to investigators. Writers of crime mysteries gave their readers superstar sleuths who could mete out justice through their uncanny ability to observe and piece together the smallest clues.

A sleuth can be referred to as a detective, gumshoe (wearing sneaker-like shoes, enabling them to sneak around quietly), private investigator (PI), or chief inspector. But they are also commonly called Sherlock, and association comes directly from author Arthur Conan

Doyle, whose character Sherlock Holmes has become the literary world's most well-known sleuth.

Doyle's Sherlock Holmes stories are narrated by Holmes's investigative partner, Dr. John Watson. Doyle immediately introduces us to Sherlock's incredible powers of deduction upon the very first meeting of Holmes and Dr. Watson in *A Study in Scarlet* (1887). Sherlock shakes Dr. Watson's hand and says, "How are you? . . . You have been to Afghanistan, I perceive."

"How on earth did you know that?" an astonished Dr. Watson replies.

Not bad from a single handshake, huh?

But despite Sherlock Holmes's sharp and intuitive mind, Doyle also paints him throughout the many stories as quite human. That starts with Holmes's drug problem. The second Sherlock Holmes book, *The Sign of the Four* (1890), begins with Dr. Watson explicitly describing the depths of Sherlock's addiction:

> Sherlock Holmes took his bottle from the corner of the mantel-piece and his hypodermic syringe from its neat morocco case. With his long, white, nervous fingers he adjusted the delicate needle, and rolled back his left shirt-cuff. For some little time his eyes rested thoughtfully upon the sinewy forearm and wrist all dotted and scarred with innumerable puncture-marks. Finally he thrust the sharp point home, pressed down the tiny piston, and sank back into the velvet-lined armchair with a long sigh of satisfaction. . . . Three times a day for many months I had witnessed this performance, but custom had not reconciled my mind to it.

It also can be very difficult for readers to reconcile the two faces of Sherlock Holmes, but that duality is part of what makes Doyle's character so compelling, and the author made sure to bring his drug problem front and center in the opening of Holmes's second case.

ENCYCLOPEDIA B.

Want your mysteries solved by a ten-year-old? Try Leroy "Encyclopedia" Brown, the creation of author Donald Sobol. No murders here, mind you. The sleuth, who is aided by his slightly older assistant and bodyguard Sally Kimball, works out of his parents' garage and advertises his services to the neighborhood: "25 cents per day, plus expenses—No case too small." Of course, Encyclopedia (a nickname referring to his knowledge of vast subjects) Brown also helps out his dad, the local police chief, on occasion.

Sobol starts out his story *Encyclopedia Brown Gets His Man* (1967) with these lines: "The Idaville police department has an excellent record, but that's because the chief of police's ten-year-old son is Encyclopedia Brown. People praise Chief Brown, and Chief Brown doesn't feel like he can admit how much help his son gives him because he doubts anyone would believe him." It's a perfectly penned opening to impress upon an audience this youngster's prowess as a sleuth. Also consider that line in light of the targeted readership: preteens who feel like they often know better than adults but don't get the credit they deserve.

> *Did you ever solve a mystery that no one else could? How might a ten-year-old piece together clues differently than an adult?*

TEEN SLEUTHS

Publisher Edward Stratemeyer created a pair of teen detective franchises: the Hardy Boys (1927) and Nancy Drew (1930). The Hardy Boys, teenage brothers Frank and Joe, are amateur sleuths who solve complex cases that their older and more experienced counterparts cannot. The teen tandem proved so popular that Stratemeyer decided to next star a lone female, Nancy Drew, in a similar role. Who were the authors responsible for these literary successes? It's difficult to say because over the years, a slew of ghostwriters contributed to the more than 350 combined books that comprise the two series. A pseudonym, or pen name, is ascribed to each franchise. The author of the Hardy Boys is the fictitious Franklin W. Dixon, while the name Carolyn Keene was chosen to represent the author of Nancy Drew.

NINE

TRUE LOVE AND HEARTBREAK

FEUDING FAMILIES

William Shakespeare penned the world's most recognized pair of star-crossed lovers in *The Tragedy of Romeo and Juliet* (1597), from his tragic play of the same name. The duo, synonymous with both one another and the idealism of true love, has stepped off the pages of a play and into our society. Think of all the times you've heard someone say, "He's a real Romeo" or "They're a pair of star-crossed lovers."

Sixteen-year-old Romeo Montague and thirteen-year-old Juliet Capulet meet, fall in love, and then get secretly married. Why in secrecy? The Montague and Capulet families are sworn enemies. Couldn't the relationship between Romeo and Juliet soften the feud? Any thought of that goes out the window when Romeo kills Juliet's cousin in a sword fight.

Romeo's opening line, before he has ever met Juliet, is a reply to his cousin bidding him good morning: "Is the day so young?" A despondent Romeo is just coming off a bad breakup. His reply is also significant because this play is a tragedy and Romeo's young life is in peril. It's a response to which we can all relate, thinking the end of our last relationship feels like the end of the world.

Is Romeo quick to fall in love? Absolutely. Often women are the ones depicted as overly emotional. Therefore, Romeo may seem rather whiny as a romantic. And remember, this is a theater production, and the audience desires action at a quick pace.

Here is Romeo's speech after simply glimpsing Juliet for the first time:

> O, she doth teach the torches to burn bright!
> It seems she hangs upon the cheek of night...
> Did my heart love till now?

This is the same Romeo who, earlier that very day, was lamenting his lost love. *What was her name?* All this and he and Juliet haven't even spoken yet!

However, they speak a moment later, and Romeo is not shy about his feelings. Romeo wants to kiss her. Juliet plays it cool by telling him that "lips" are best used for "prayer." But they do kiss twice, in public, with Juliet's family eyeing the scene. It's an amazing first meeting and opening set of lines, with descriptions and dialogue to hasten an enthralled audience forward.

STREETLIGHT SERENADE

Scottish singer/songwriter Mark Knopfler uses Shakespeare's *Romeo and Juliet* as the framework for a song about a failed romance. His piece is also appropriately titled "Romeo and Juliet" (1980). (Did you know that titles aren't protected by copyright?)

Knopfler's melodic opening lines quickly align his protagonist with the famous play:

> A lovestruck Romeo sings the streets a serenade
> Laying everybody low with a love song that he made

Shakespeare's Romeo is known for his poetic speech. Knopfler's speaker is a songwriter. But unlike Shakespeare's tragic play, in which only death ultimately unites the pair, Knopfler's Juliet has completely moved on from her love affair with Romeo.

This song is set in modern times, so as Romeo "finds a streetlight," stepping out of the shade to reveal himself beneath Juliet's window, she responds by singing a verse from a 1960s hit song containing the lyric "My boyfriend's back and you're gonna be in trouble," perhaps warning Romeo that she's now with someone else. Stinging Romeo even more deeply, though, Juliet has publicly proclaimed, "Oh, Romeo, yeah, you know I used to have a scene with him." That's about as cold as it gets.

But Romeo's stuck in the past, reminding Juliet, "You said I love you like the stars above, I'll love you 'til I die." Knopfler's opening line describes Romeo as "lovestruck," and the songwriter wasn't kidding around. Ever the optimist for love, this Romeo believes there's still a glimmer of hope for the former couple:

> Juliet, I'd do the stars with you any time . . .
> "You and me, babe, how about it?"

FAIRY-TALE ROMANCE

Shakespeare has been credited with coining an abundance of words and phrases in our current lexicon. His linguistic contributions include *uncomfortable, fashionable, all that glitters is not gold, cold-blooded, swagger, break the ice, fair play*, and many more—as well as the name *Jessica*, which didn't exist as a female name prior to Shakespeare's invention of it. However, one common phrase that usually starts a story, and often a fairy tale, was definitely not invented by Shakespeare: "Once upon a time," which predates Shakespeare by almost two centuries.

Why do so many writers begin with "Once upon a time"? After all, it's rather imprecise. It doesn't provide the reader with a date, time, or even era. But that vagueness is actually the strength behind it and why it is almost exclusively used for fiction. It's a signal for the audience to engage their imagination and find a place in their mind to allow the forthcoming story to occur.

Singer/songwriter Taylor Swift wonderfully uses the phrase to open her song "I Knew You Were Trouble" (2021):

> Once upon a time, a few mistakes ago
> I was in your sights

Was this relationship gone sour ever a fairy tale? And if so, from the perspective of whom?

"A few mistakes ago," provides the listener with another vague time stamp, though one seemingly closer to right now. It might also infer that the narrator has gained some added experience through the recognition of these mistakes and could be looking back with wiser eyes. The addition of "I was in your sights," makes it sound as if the narrator had been nothing more than an appealing target for this former romantic flame.

Here's direct proof of that, appearing later in the lyrics:

A new notch in your belt is all I'll ever be.

So the opening line, despite its impreciseness, is actually quite informative. The refrain reminds us that the narrator should have known better then, but she certainly does now:

I knew you were trouble when you walked in . . .
Trouble, trouble, trouble

Hey, maybe he had hella-good hair.

DID HE OR DIDN'T HE?

Did Shakespeare ever use the phrase *once upon a time*? The answer is a definite maybe. You see, in the Shakespearean play *The Tempest* (c. 1610–1611), one of the characters, in trying to frame a reference point, says, "When time was." The footnotes, which help to clarify any confusing early modern English, sometimes translate this as "once upon a time." So the answer is . . . a definite maybe.

LOVE WITHOUT OBLIGATION

Songwriter John Hartford (1937–2001) was a steamboat pilot and musician who accompanied himself incredibly on percussion. He'd play either the banjo or fiddle while standing on a plywood board and wearing tap shoes. With a mic beside the board, Hartford's tap dancing sounded like rhythmic drumming.

Hartford wrote a song called "Gentle on My Mind" (1967) about a drifter whose true love doesn't saddle him with obligations, instead accepting and loving the drifter without trying to change or tie him down. The piece's perfectly penned opening line is

It's knowin' that your door is always open
And your path is free to walk
That tends to make me leave my sleepin' bag
Rolled up and stashed behind your couch

The speaker seems always ready to move on to someplace new, even when he's spending precious time with his true love. It's a simple line that encapsulates what some might perceive as an easygoing yet complicated relationship.

Marriage? Their relationship isn't bound by the "ink stains that have dried upon some line." And whenever they're apart, which might be most of the time, the speaker muses, distance doesn't diminish his feelings.

"Though the wheat fields and the clotheslines / and the junkyards and the highways come between us," the speaker can still simply close his eyes and see his love "movin' on the backroads by the rivers of my memory / And for hours you're just gentle on my mind."

The song is a celebration of a love without boundaries or borders.

LOVE AND MARRIAGE

English novelist Jane Austen (1775–1817) focused much of her writing on the idea of how love and marriage were viewed during an era in which almost all women depended on men for financial support. Her novel *Pride and Prejudice* (1813) examines the journey of five single sisters whose parents view them partly as possessions to be married off into the proper circumstances to secure their futures. Sounds a lot like love is taking a back seat to a title and bank account.

Austen's opening line reinforces the wide acceptance of a businesslike aspect to marriage: "It is a truth universally acknowledged, that a single man in possession of a good fortune must be in want of a wife." It's a stereotype that seems to shortchange everyone involved.

But the novel does present a character of internal rebellion. The second-eldest of the Bennet sisters, Elizabeth, the story's main protagonist, has a keen and growing awareness of self. And during a time when many women desperately hoped to receive a marriage proposal,

Elizabeth rejects a pair of such proposals. And she had no idea that one of those proposals was about to happen. Can you imagine being *totally* shocked by a marriage proposal? Wouldn't you be in a relationship that progressed over time, giving you at least some clue? Arranged marriages still exist today in many cultures. Only Austen paints the upper-crust Brits of this era as being exceedingly businesslike about it.

"I am only resolved to act in that manner, which will, in my own opinion, constitute my happiness, without reference to you, or to any person so wholly unconnected with me," Elizabeth tells a woman of greater social standing than herself, who voices an opinion on Elizabeth's marriage choices. It was a societal structure that could perhaps make today's forty-page prenuptial agreements appear intimate and charming.

CAN'T YOU HEAR ME?

Poet Donika Ross Kelly paints a picture of unrequited love on the high seas in the remarkable piece "Love Poem: Mermaid" (2016). Sirens are mythical female creatures who sing a song so tempting at sea that sailors, following their alluring voices, often sink their ships on the jagged rocks from which these sirens call. They are, in a sense, closely related to mermaids, who possess the upper body of a human and the tail of a fish.

In Kelly's poem, the speaker spots what she believes to be another of her own kind and falls in love at first sight—only it's actually a figurehead, a wooden carving representing a woman attached to the prow (the portion of a ship's bow, or leading edge, that rests above the waterline). Many figureheads are a seminaked bare-breasted women with flowing hair, representing a goddess with the power to calm the uncertain seas ahead.

The poem begins with the speaker calling to the object of her affection,

> Do you ever look into a mirror,
> which is also an ocean heavy with sun?

An opening line searching for a common bond as a conversation starter? Is the siren lonely? Perhaps so because she lures sailors to their deaths. Is it possible that because of her effect on men, she could only have a relationship with another siren or mermaid?

Of course, there is no response from the mute and unfeeling carving:

> I have claimed this rock,
> which is also your heart

Is there any hope for a relationship here?

"O that my voice / were a knife," muses the speaker—perhaps the only way to separate the figurehead from her ship. But the speaker is left sadly alone, wishing from her rock that "there was nothing / between us but salt and breath."

HOLDING NOTHING BACK

Singer/songwriter Janis Ian attended the New York City High School of Music and Art. Her first hit song came at the age of fourteen. Ian eventually went on to pen an anthem for teens who felt socially isolated with "At Seventeen" (1975). It's a song about desperately wanting a first romantic relationship and to be accepted by one's peers.

Ian's opening line is startlingly frank and brutal:

> I learned the truth at seventeen
> That love is meant for beauty queens
> And high school girls with clear-skinned smiles

That narrow definition leaves out a lot of teens, including "those of us with ravaged faces / Lacking in the social graces," for whom Ian sings.

Nothing is sidestepped or out of bounds, with the songwriter detailing great emotional disappointments:

> To those of us who knew the pain
> Of valentines that never came

The idea of "your time will come," emerging one day as a beautiful swan in full control of your life, is viewed as something with little to no relevance in combating what many isolated teens feel at the moment:

> When dreams were all they gave for free
> To ugly duckling girls like me . . .
> At seventeen

"To write something that honest and open was really difficult," noted Ian.

> From the first line off, I knew that I was taking on something and I wasn't sure I was ready for it. I had never heard anything that talked that blatantly about feeling ugly or feeling unwanted. Other songs touched on it, but they usually had a happy ending. And I was determined that "At Seventeen" wouldn't have a happy ending. It wouldn't say, "Then I grew up and I became beautiful and I lost weight and my skin cleared up and everything was fine." I wanted it to stay true to itself, and it took a long time to write it.[1]

CONSTANTLY PARODIED

We've seen a good bit of love gone wrong in this chapter, so let's end on a supremely positive note with a poem you've probably already heard, in one form or another: "How Do I Love Thee?" (Sonnet 43; 1850) by Elizabeth Barrett Browning. (No, she's not the protagonist from *Pride and Prejudice*. The names just happen to be similar.) She wrote it for her husband Robert Browning, also a writer.

The poem begins,

> How do I love thee? Let me count the ways.
> I love thee to the depth and breadth and height
> My soul can reach

It's a magnificent opening, bringing together the physical and spiritual. It's so good, in fact, that you've probably heard it being parodied hundreds of times—from cartoons to greeting cards to rom-coms (romantic comedies).

One of the better-known parodies comes from the teen rom-com *10 Things I Hate about You* (1999), which is a modernized version of the Shakespeare (you can't avoid this guy) play *The Taming of the Shrew* (1594). The female lead, Kat Stratford, played by Julia Stiles, delivers a version of Browning's sonnet to her male counterpart, Patrick Verona (that's the hometown of Romeo and Juliet), played by Heath Ledger. She starts, "I hate the way you talk to me and the way you cut your hair." It sounds like it's going to be an onslaught of insults. Only the piece quickly changes to some hidden positive feelings over the course of just a few lines, perhaps hinting at budding true love: "But mostly I hate the way I don't hate you.... Not even a little bit. Not even at all."

This movie scene, cowritten by Karen McCullah and Kristen Smith and staged almost 140 years after Browning's death, only exists because of her perfectly penned opening line in "How Do I Love Thee?"

> *Did you ever write your own parody of something recognizable? You've already witnessed* The Simpsons *do it with Edgar Allan Poe's "The Raven" and the movie* Spaceballs' *parody of the sci-fi classic* Star Wars. *The simplest way to begin is to borrow the opening line from something iconic, something people will recognize, and go in a different direction with it. Try it! I'll bet the finished piece will make your friends and family laugh and smile.*

TEN

ORATORS AND FAMOUS SPEECHES

Being a writer enables you to express yourself and connect with others—through ideas, emotions, and even the audience's imagination. But there are also writers who possess a dual talent: to be able to compose powerful ideas and then deliver them to an audience via their own voice.

"Of all the talents bestowed upon [us], none is so precious as the gift of oratory. He who enjoys it wields a power more durable than that of a great king. He is an independent force in the world," said Winston Churchill, the two-time prime minister of the United Kingdom, whose stirring speeches rallied British citizens through their darkest hours during World War II as they were fighting the Nazi regime's unceasing bombing of their cities. Can speech inspire people to actions and unwavering resolve?

Throughout history, the *right words*, delivered at the *right time* by the *right speaker*, have motivated people to stand up to enormous hardships and ultimately succeed in their struggle. In this chapter, I present the opening lines of several famous speeches delivered by extraordinary voices and explain how those lines set the tone for what would follow.

GALVANIZING WORDS

"Four score and seven years ago our fathers brought forth on this continent, a new nation, conceived in Liberty, and dedicated to the proposition that all men are created equal." That's President Abraham Lincoln's opening line to the Gettysburg Address, a speech consisting of just ten sentences. But don't confuse length with importance.

President Lincoln delivered the speech on November 19, 1863, during the US Civil War (1861–1865), at the Soldier's National Cemetery in Gettysburg, Pennsylvania, just several months after Union forces defeated the Confederates there in what would prove to be the deadliest battle of the conflict, with more than 50,000 casualties and more than 7,000 fatalities.

The opening line is arguably the most recognizable sentence in US history. A score is twenty, so four score and seven years ago is eighty-seven years. That brings us back to 1776—the birth of this nation and the Declaration of Independence, which states, "All men are created equal."

Lincoln was leaning on our proud history to connect to his audience. It was a time when the Americans fought together to oppose the British, instead of fighting against one another. He was also reminding the listener that the concept of slavery flies in the face of the ideals on which the United States was founded. It is an opening line almost without parallel.

Lincoln went on to say, "The world will little note, nor long remember what we say here." He was wrong about that because his speech has endured to this day.

Would America even survive this terrible Civil War? In considering that question, Lincoln spoke about the soldiers who died on that very battlefield: "We here highly resolve that these dead shall not have died in vain—that this nation, under God, shall have a new birth of freedom—and that government of the people, by the people, for the people, shall not perish from the earth." It is an ending equal to the depth of Lincoln's beginning and therefore a stirring masterpiece of the English language.

Sadly, there are no actual recordings of Lincoln's voice. He was assassinated twelve years before Edison invented his phonograph with its play-back sound.

> *When you read lines from the Gettysburg Address in your head, how do you imagine Lincoln's voice? What qualities of sound would you assign it?*

LIBERTY OR DEATH

On the cusp of the American Revolution, Patrick Henry, on March 23, 1775, spoke at the Second Virginia Convention to rouse his fellow Virginians to arms against the British. Henry followed other speakers who did not share his view. Therefore, his opening line was polite and tactful because he knew that he would need their support in the near future: "Different men often see the same subject in different lights; and, therefore, I hope it will not be thought disrespectful to those gentlemen if, entertaining as I do, opinions of a character very opposite to theirs, I shall speak forth my sentiments freely, and without reserve."

Henry, a gifted orator, succinctly spoke about the unfairness of life under British rule, including the colonies being taxed without proper representation. But by the end of his speech, Henry shifted from details to pure emotions, undoubtedly building confidence in his listeners of a like mind and maybe swaying those Virginians still sitting on the fence, waiting to lean one way or another: "Why stand we here idle? . . . Is life so dear, or peace so sweet, as to be purchased at the price of chains and slavery? . . . I know not what course others may take; but as for me, give me liberty or give me death!" Patrick Henry was all in, with a public declaration against King George III.

A DECLARATION

Stirring speeches, like that of Patrick Henry, eventually led to revolution and the penning of the Declaration of Independence, which was unanimously adopted by Congress on July 4, 1776. The document was drafted by Thomas Jefferson and then edited by several others, including Benjamin Franklin and John Adams.

It begins, "We hold these truths to be self-evident, that all men are created equal, that they are endowed by their Creator with certain unalienable Rights, that among these are Life, Liberty and the pursuit of Happiness." That's a line that has so far stood the test of time.

It's extremely difficult for a speech to be emotional from the first word to the last, so by starting off in a calm and reserved manner, Henry gave himself the space to gather serious momentum. The next time you consider his speech's famous final words "Give me liberty or give me death!" understand that they are perfectly counterbalanced by the tone and tenor of his opening line.

THE VOICE OF YOUTH

Malala Yousafzai, a Pakistani by birth and worldwide activist for female education, is the youngest Nobel Peace Prize recipient (she was awarded at age seventeen). Two years prior, at age fifteen, she was shot, along with two other girls, by terrorists in an assassination attempt to silence her voice. Yousafzai was struck in the head by a bullet and remained in critical condition for some time before eventually making a complete recovery. The terrorist attempt on Yousafzai's life only served to bring more attention to her cause. The memoir *I Am Malala: The Girl Who Stood Up for Education and Was Shot by the Taliban*, authored by Yousafzai and Christina Lamb, resonated with readers around the globe.

In July 2013, Yousafzai addressed the United Nations Youth Assembly in New York. Her speech began (after her thanks to everyone), "Dear brothers and sisters, do remember one thing: Malala Day is not my day. Today is the day of every woman, every boy and every girl who have raised their voice for their rights."

Yousafzai's choice of opening lines serves to magnify the significance of her story and where she stands. It is not Malala alone to whom we are listening. She is just the one standing at the microphone. There could be a line of several million standing behind her waiting to tell their story. And in actuality, there is: "So here I stand, one girl, among many. I speak not for myself, but so those without a voice can be heard. Those who have fought for their rights. . . . Their right to equality of opportunity . . . to be educated."

It is a brilliantly conceived speech delivered with poise and passion by someone in their teens. *Author! Author!*

I HAVE A DREAM

On August 28, 1963, Martin Luther King Jr. delivered his iconic "I Have a Dream" speech at the Lincoln Memorial in Washington, DC. The setting of that occasion, the March on Washington for Jobs and Freedom, provided King an opportunity to channel the words and deeds of Abraham Lincoln. King's speech started, "Five score years ago, a great American, in whose symbolic shadow we stand today, signed the Emancipation Proclamation. This momentous decree came as a great beacon light of hope to millions of Negro slaves who had been seared in the flames of withering injustice.... But 100 years later, the Negro still is not free."

It mirrors Lincoln's Gettysburg Address by using the word *score*. In this case, the Emancipation Proclamation was signed one hundred years prior. It's a sensational opening relating directly to the grounds—the Lincoln Memorial—where approximately 250,000 supporters were standing and listening.

King then harkened back to the words of the Declaration of Independence in laying out his premise:

> When the architects of our republic wrote the magnificent words of the Constitution and the Declaration of Independence, they were signing a promissory note to which every American was to fall heir. This note was a promise that all men—yes, Black men as well as white men—would be guaranteed the unalienable rights of life, liberty and the pursuit of happiness.

After a few sections, King subtly shifted focus. It can easily be argued that his speech has two separate sets of opening lines. The first set is about circumstance. The second set is about passionate hope, signaled by the line "I have a dream."

The orator used the phrase *I have a dream* eight times in a matter of minutes, much like the refrain of a song, sticking in the audience's mind and memory. It's a technique called anaphora, used by speakers and writers for emphasis and unity. King then connected the repeated statement to commonly shared desires, making it much more personal for both himself and the audience: "I have a dream that my four little children will one day live in a nation where they will not be judged by the color of their skin but by the content of their character. I have a dream today."

Then came a second powerful refrain in "Let freedom ring," which he used to unite a cross-section of the country: "So let freedom ring from the prodigious hilltops of New Hampshire . . . the mighty mountains of New York . . . the snowcapped Rockies of Colorado . . . the curvaceous slopes of California."

King's ending is powerful, calling on faith to further unite the listeners: "When we allow freedom ring . . . all of God's children . . . will be able to join hands and sing . . . Free at last. Free at Last. Thank God Almighty, we are free at last." It is simply one of history's most poignant and important speeches.

NO MORE, FOREVER

Chief Joseph of the Nez Perce led a Native American resistance in the Pacific Northwest after his people were removed from their ancestral homes by the US government. Along with a band of approximately eight hundred natives, Chief Joseph was pursued by and fought the US Army while he was trying to reach Canada to seek political asylum for his people.

When there was no hope remaining for his people, Chief Joseph delivered a short surrender speech to his US Army counterpart in October 1877. He began, "I am tired of fighting." A singular line echoed throughout history near the end of almost every violent conflict or war, conveying the futility and wastefulness of battle. And it absolutely sets the tone for what's to come.

He then detailed the pain and loss suffered by his people: "It is cold and we have no blankets. The little children are freezing to death." The speech ended as powerfully as it started, with Chief Joseph's personal plea for peace: "Hear me, my chiefs. I am tired; my heart is sick and sad. From where the sun now stands I will fight no more forever."

Remember, there was no mass media in this time, just the telegraph and the telephone, which had been invented the year before and did not yet have a large network. For the most part, word of the surrender spread by horseback.

HEATING THINGS UP

Greta Thunberg's climate activism began at home in Sweden, when she persuaded her parents to reduce the carbon footprint in their household. Thunberg then began skipping school at the age of fifteen—her own personal school strike—to protest outside the Swedish Parliament, demanding they take action on climate change. Her message resonated with many across the globe. One year later, in 2019, Thunberg was invited to speak at the United Nations' Climate Action Summit in New York City.

Thunberg's no-nonsense opening line set the tone for her blunt and straightforward content: "My message is that we'll be watching you." This opening warns, "You have responsibility past today. We won't be leaving here proud of ourselves for simply pushing the issue. We want results, and voting you out of office is very possible."

Thunberg then challenged an assemblage of world leaders to be more responsible, calling them out for dragging their feet for too long in addressing this issue: "I shouldn't be up here. I should be back in school. . . . Yet you all come to us young people for hope. How dare you!"

Most speeches seek to establish an early connection between people who might want to approach a problem differently (remember Patrick Henry's opening tact?). But not Thunberg's: "Entire ecosystems are collapsing. We are in the beginning of a mass extinction, and all you can talk about is money. . . . How dare you!" (Similar to the repetition in Martin Luther King Jr.'s "I Have a Dream" speech).

But even Thunberg understood that on some level she needed to extend a symbolic olive branch to those currently in power, who could facilitate climate solutions the quickest: "If you really understood the situation and still kept on failing to act, then you would be evil. And that I refuse to believe."

After her speech had concluded, Thunberg's haunting opening line undoubtedly echoed in the ears of many who possessed the power to make changes: "We'll be watching you."

> Consider Thunberg's and Yousafzai's impact on the world. Do you believe that young people who may not even be old enough to vote can be important cogs in creating change in the world on issues on which they hold a passionate belief?

HEARTFELT FAREWELL

It was an era without social media, so superstar athletes weren't necessarily polished when it came to public speaking. But that didn't hinder New York Yankees first baseman Lou Gehrig from delivering a humble and heartfelt speech in front of nearly 60,000 fans at Yankee Stadium on a somber July afternoon in 1939.

Gehrig, nicknamed the "Iron Horse" because of his incredible durability, played 2,130 consecutive games. Suddenly, in the prime of Gehrig's life, his on-field performance and health started to fail due to an unknown ailment. Gehrig was soon diagnosed with amyotrophic lateral sclerosis (ALS), an incurable neuromuscular disorder. At age thirty-six, he was forced to retire.

His farewell speech to the fans in attendance began, "For the past two weeks you have been reading about a bad break. Yet today, I consider myself the luckiest man on the face of the Earth." As he paused, the reverberating echo through the stadium sound system seemingly repeated his now fabled second sentence. "I consider myself the luckiest man on the face of the Earth."

It was an opening that affirmed Gehrig didn't want anyone to waste their time pitying him because his life had been filled with incredible associations—loved ones, teammates, friends, and fans, many of whom Gehrig mentioned specifically by name in his next few lines: "So I close in saying that I might have been given a bad break, but I've got an awful lot to live for. Thank you." If Gehrig's goal was to ease the tensions and concerns of others while showing how grateful he was for their unwavering support, he accomplished that with a grand-slam speech.

Sadly, Gehrig passed away two years later. ALS is now commonly referred to in the United States as Lou Gehrig's disease.

ELEVEN

PERSPECTIVE

All artists create with a perspective—the way they personally see things and the way they want to influence their audience's view. There are times when the perspective of an artist is purposefully ambiguous, with the goal of not trying to lead the audience in a particular direction or to a desired conclusion. Obviously, each audience member brings their own unique perspective to a work, as well.

In this chapter, I present a number of works that celebrate the idea of perspective in different ways. They are pieces that on some level should make you think, evaluating how both you and the artist might view certain subjects; there might even be a blending of those perspectives, leaving you with a new viewpoint that you never experienced before. Wouldn't that be interesting!

JUST IMAGINE

Liverpool-born singer/songwriter John Lennon first came to prominence as a member of the Beatles (spelled like a musical beat, not the insect), often coauthoring songs with bandmate Paul McCartney. But on his 1971 solo album, Lennon penned the title track "Imagine" with his wife Yoko Ono.

The song is a magnificent lyrical expression based solely on perspective. It starts,

> Imagine there's no heaven
> It's easy if you try

That line angered some listeners and faith-based organizations. The thought that there was no heaven had them fuming. But Lennon's song never claimed such a thing. He simply said, *imagine* the possibility.

The first line artfully opens the doors to a myriad of other imagined possibilities, with the word *imagine* repeated for emphasis:

Imagine there's no countries...
And no religion, too...
Imagine no possessions

Individual perspective soon turns to broad inclusion as Lennon reaches out to listeners of a like mind, even if the idealism expressed in the lyrics is something most people never believed could become a reality:

I hope someday you'll join us
And the world will live as one

And no, John Lennon himself never gave away all his earthly possessions (cars, mansions, money, etc.). Hypocritical on Lennon's part or just an idyllic piece of writing to make you consider the world with a new perspective?

SCRAMBLED EGGS

Perspective plays a major role in the Beatles' song "Yesterday" (1965), which is credited to the collaborative team of Lennon–McCartney. But in actuality, the song was written by Paul McCartney, who claims to have woken from a dream with the melody ringing in his ears. Before McCartney had lyrics, he sang the words *scrambled eggs*, which is the same number of syllables as *yesterday*, as a placeholder while the lyrical story was being fashioned.

At first listen, "Yesterday" feels like a song solely about a crushing blow dealt by lost love. But there's a subtle undertow of perspective that gives it even more depth. McCartney's opening lines are,

> Yesterday
> All my troubles seemed so far away
> Now it looks as though they're here to stay

Yesterday gives the piece an incredible sense of immediacy. It was all there in the speaker's hands and heart less than twenty-four hours ago. But take note of the words *seemed* and *as though*, letting us know that this is the interpretation of the speaker, his singular perspective. What happened to this vital love affair over such a short period of time?

> Why she had to go
> I don't know, she wouldn't say

We don't have her input, just the perspective of the speaker—how he feels about what's happened—as he tries to make sense of it all. And that was set up beautifully by the subtleness in personal perspective of Paul McCartney's opening two lines.

If you're not familiar with the song, listen to it. It's hard to imagine that anyone could come up with words to equally match the strength of this exquisite melody. But Paul McCartney did it, with a little help from his friends: *scrambled eggs*. Accepting that type of challenge is what being an artist is all about.

THE BEST AND WORST

How long can one person with a full plate of food hold off four people who are really hungry, who are, in some cases, starving? Certainly not forever. The French Revolution of the late eighteenth century is the backdrop for Charles Dickens's historical novel *A Tale of Two Cities* (1859). Every revolution centers on perspective: the perspective held by the powerful as opposed to that of the powerless wanting to change their position in life.

Dickens describes the differences in daily life and social justice for French peasants, who made up approximately four-fifths of the population, as opposed to that of the middle class and France's elite ruling class, with the vast majority of the country's wealth disproportionately controlled by the elite. The author's opening lines, among the most recognizable in literature, perfectly reflect this dual perspective among the citizens of France: "It was the best of times, it was the worst of times, it was the age of wisdom, it was the age of foolishness, it was the epoch of belief, it was the epoch of incredulity, it was the season of Light, it was the season of Darkness, it was the spring of hope, it was the winter of despair, we had everything before us, we had nothing before us."

Dickens is using a technique called antithesis, comparing opposites and extremes. And when those differences become imbedded within a society, a revolt is usually in the air. Dickens' opening lines absolutely prepare us for the societal upheaval to come. "Liberty! Equality! Fraternity!" is what the revolutionaries chanted—in French, naturally.

A MORE PERSONAL PERSPECTIVE

Dickens's opening line to *A Tale of Two Cities* was echoed more than a century later in singer/songwriter Billy Joel's "Summer, Highland Falls" (1976), only instead of the notion of the best and the worst being cast onto a historical event, Joel writes about those conditions as they pertain to his own life, especially as an artist. His song begins,

> They say that these are not the best of times
> But they're the only times I've ever known

The songwriter discusses the difficulties of life and relationships, focusing on the idea that our individual triumphs and failures, no matter how small, can provide huge swings in feelings and perceptions:

> For we are always what our situations hand us
> It's either sadness or euphoria

"Sadness" or "euphoria"—two far-reaching extremes.

How do we deal emotionally and psychologically with our ever-changing outcomes? Joel terms that tightrope "the ledges of our lives" that we're forced to walk without a safety net on a day when the wind can kick up at any moment:

> Our reason coexists with our insanity
> And though we choose between reality and madness
> It's either sadness or euphoria

Joel's opening line sets the tone that we have little choice in the matter, except maybe to simply make do the best that we can. "Most artists—a lot of composers, a lot of painters, people who create—have tendencies of manic depression. We go up. We go down. We have these incredible euphoric highs. We have these depressed lows. And if we can utilize them as artists it's good. If we can't, then it's bad," noted Joel.[1]

TWO FOR ONE

Mark Twain's novel *Adventures of Huckleberry Finn* (1884) is built on perspective. But whose exactly? Huck Finn (thirteen or fourteen years old) is the narrator. Only the opening lines clearly let us know that the author is hanging directly over Huck's shoulder at all times. Huck begins, "You don't know about me without you have read a book by the name of *The Adventures of Tom Sawyer*, but that ain't no matter. That book was made by Mr. Mark Twain, and he told the truth, mainly. There was things which he stretched, but mainly he told the truth. That is nothing. I never seen anybody but lied one time or another." It's an important opening line, because for all of Huck's rough edges, he can see right from wrong and tell the truth to the reader, despite what he might say to other characters. And the reader greatly appreciates that.

Living in Missouri, a slave state at the time, Huck is nearly unaffected by the prevailing attitudes of those around him, ultimately deciding to help Jim, a runaway slave, escape. Where did Huck, a poor Anglo waif dressed in donations of oversized men's clothing, find this seemingly out-of-place perspective? The obvious answer is from "Mr. Mark Twain."

In anticipation of that connection by readers, in the preamble to his book, the author writes, "Persons attempting to find a motive in this narrative will be prosecuted; persons attempting to find a moral in it will be banished; persons attempting to find a plot in it will be shot." Another superbly crafted opening that instantly begins to influence the audience's perspective.

Psst. Mark Twain's real name is Samuel Langhorne Clemens. He was a native of Missouri and chose the pen name *Mark Twain* for a specific reason. Clemens was a riverboat pilot and the term *mark twain*, meaning water two fathoms (twelve feet) deep, is normally safe enough not to run a boat aground. And as a writer, Twain/Clemens had a habit of putting himself in deep water through his explicit social commentary.

SCRUB A WORD

Adventures of Huckleberry Finn has been challenged by many school districts for its use of the derogatory N-word. There are even several revised editions of the novel in which that term has been removed. The argument against that: Twain put that word into Huck's mouth to prove a point: that this young protagonist didn't learn such a word on his own. It was pushed on him by the surrounding society.

The novel gives us one of the most telling scenes in American literature when Huck tricks Jim into thinking he's dead, and Jim, who is inconsolable at first, realizes it was a joke and loses faith in Huck. An apology from Huck? It wasn't an easy thing to do: "It was fifteen minutes before I could work myself up to go and humble myself to a ******; but I done it, and I warn't ever sorry for it afterwards, neither. I didn't do him no more mean tricks, and I wouldn't done that one if I'd a knowed it would make him feel that way." Huck's use of that word proves that, like the society around him, he still has some things to unlearn.

BLIND FAITH

A native of Newark, New Jersey, Amiri Baraka (1934–2014), an accomplished poet, playwright, and journalist, penned "Preface to a Twenty Volume Suicide Note" (1961), a powerful poem centering on perspectives. Its title should clue you into the idea that the forthcoming speaker may be going through some tough times. The opening line reads,

> Lately, I've become accustomed to the way
> The ground opens up and envelopes me
> Each time I go out to walk the dog.

No matter the strife in the speaker's life—the helpless feeling of being small and engulfed by the world—the dog still needs to go out. There's no turning away from that responsibility and possibly others. Despite his woes, our speaker is grounded in reality, as harsh as it may be.

The speaker likes to count the stars at night, but occasionally the stars seemingly refuse to be counted. When that occurs, when there is no shining light on which to hang hopes, the speaker proceeds with an alternate plan:

> I count the holes they leave.

Why is this only a preface to a suicide note, and why will that note ultimately be twenty volumes long? Because the speaker *does* have other responsibilities beside the dog:

> I tiptoed up
> To my daughter's room and heard her
> Talking to someone.

Only the speaker could see no one else was there. It seems the youngster has her own perspective on the universe and how it can be affected. She is on her knees in prayer:

peeking into
Her own clasped hands.

And the opening line, in comparison to the closing line, lets us know that these two closely related individuals have two different points of view—perhaps because of their position, experience, or age.

PARALLEL PLAY

So the Wicked Witch, Elphaba, is green. The Good Witch, Glinda (or Galinda), is fair-skinned and blonde. How do they feel? What do they think, especially about each other? Well, if you're a fan of all things Oz, then you know that the answers to those questions are complicated. After all, we have the work of several authors, screenwriters, and playwrights to consider.

There's the original novel by L. Frank Baum, *The Wonderful Wizard of Oz* (1900); the 1939 film *The Wizard of Oz* inspired by it; and a 1978 film, *The Wiz*, with Michael Jackson playing the dancing Scarecrow and Diana Ross as Dorothy. Then there's Gregory Maguire's novel *Wicked: The Life and Times of the Wicked Witch of the West* (1995) and the 2003 musical *Wicked*, loosely based on that book.

Perhaps the most interesting moment between Elphaba and Galinda comes when they're teenagers and assigned to be roommates at Shiz University ("Where knowledge meets magic!") in *Wicked*. The equally disappointed pair shares a parallel perspective in their immediate dislike for one another. Their feelings are wonderfully examined as they sing a duet, which lyricist Stephen Schwartz crafted in the form of a letter home through the song "What Is This Feeling?" Take note of the way each character addresses their parents.

The semivacuous Galinda begins her salutation, "Dearest, darlingest Momsie and Popsicle." (If your father is a Popsicle, does that mean you treat others coldly? Just asking.) The serious Elphaba, though, starts with a more formal "My dear father."

They look each other over and register virtually the same complaint in depicting their unacceptable new roomie.

"Unusually and exceedingly peculiar / And altogether quite impossible to describe," sings Galinda, who doesn't mention Elphaba's skin tone.

The direct Elphaba simply states, "Blonde."

What singular word best describes the mutual feelings? *Loathing*, an intense dislike; disgust; and, yes, even hatred.

In two-part harmony, they sing about the other,

> Let's just say
> I loathe it all
> Every little trait, however small
> Makes my very flesh begin to crawl

But a baseless "unadulterated loathing" such as this is hard to maintain, and their relationship really has nowhere to go but up—whether on a broom (Elphaba) or a floating bubble (Galinda). And their future interactions become a lot more interesting and nuanced and present multiple perspectives.

> *Did you ever develop a close friendship with someone whom you did not like at first? If so, what was the turning point in that relationship?*

SLIPPER TRIVIA

I want you to be the smartest person in the room, so here's a bit of trivia about the Land of Oz. In the 1939 movie *The Wizard of Oz*, Dorothy's slippers are ruby red, but in L. Frank Baum's original novel *The Wonderful Wizard of Oz*, they are silver. It seems MGM, the studio that made the movie, wanted a brighter color. That way the slippers would really pop on the screen during the parts filmed in Technicolor. The slippers are silver in *Wicked*, though, with the musical paying homage to Baum's vision.

MEASURE OF A YEAR

Jonathan Larson wrote the 1996 musical *Rent*, inspired by the Italian opera *La Bohème*, which is set in Paris. It was Larson's passion to marry classic theater with pop and rock music. He staged his version in Manhattan's East Village, with the HIV/AIDS epidemic substituting for the severe tuberculosis outbreak in the late nineteenth century.

The cast is comprised primarily of artists trying desperately to make a living through their talents and, yes, pay the rent. But for Larson, the word *rent* also means *torn*. Several characters are either HIV-positive or have AIDS and are struggling with their health. They're torn over many things, including family, romantic relationships, and the idealism of their art.

That's why the song that traditionally opens the second act, "Seasons of Love," speaks to so many people. The opening line is iconic, breaking down the length of a year into minutes. Amazingly, it goes from being a snappy counting chore to something exquisitely personal and meaningful:

525,600 minutes
525,000 moments so dear

The line poses the question of what time is worth in the framework of our lives. Has it been well spent or wasted? It's the "so dear" that adds depth and guides the audience from their minds to their hearts.

So the question arises both for the characters and the audience:

How do you measure, measure a year in the life?
In daylights, sunsets, in midnights, in cups of coffee
In inches, in miles, in laughter, in strife

The perspectives can be wide and varied. Part of the power of the writing is that the entire cast sings the song together, with the audience debating the answer internally. Larson's lyrical answer via a chorus, informing us that we "measure in love," undoubtedly finds room in everyone's perspective.

Tragically, Larson died unexpectedly at age thirty-five from a misdiagnosed heart problem, just one day before *Rent* was to have its preview opening. To honor Larson, the cast performed "Seasons of Love" to start the show that evening.

Overture. Curtains. Lights.

TWELVE

YOUNG ADULTS

Young people, both teens and preteens, make incredible protagonists in stories, poems, films, and other forms of expression. Why? Well, they basically have the same problems, hopes, and dreams as adults, but teens and preteens normally have much less power and fewer resources to address them. That fundamentally makes these characters somewhat dependent on others, such as family, friends, and teachers. But a young adult protagonist who overcomes that lack of power and maybe even uses their age to an advantage makes a major impression on the audience, and we often become their biggest cheering section.

So let's take a look at some important young adult characters and the artistic works in which they reside. And let's see how the writer chooses to start their stories, reflecting the protagonist's age, dilemmas, and goals.

UNFORTUNATELY INTRIGUING

Author Daniel Handler, who uses the pen name Lemony Snicket, has written a much-beloved series of books beneath the banner *A Series of Unfortunate Events* (1999–2006). The protagonists are a trio of orphaned siblings, Violet (age fourteen); Klaus (age twelve); and the infant Sunny, who, though she speaks in baby-talk, has advanced skills and the makings of becoming a great detective one day (move over Maggie Simpson!). They are *unfortunately* in the custody of Count Olaf, a distant relative and failed actor who is after the fortune left to the three children by their deceased parents.

Here are the opening two lines to the first book in the series: "If you are interested in stories with happy endings, you would be better off reading some other book. In this book, not only is there no happy ending, there is no happy beginning and very few happy things in the middle." Why is this opening so beautifully orchestrated?

The author is basically challenging you to put the book down and go read something else, but it's done in such an engaging way—using hyperbole, an over exaggeration (in this case, stating that nothing good will happen at any point in the story). The reader intuitively really wants to hang around and prove that the author's claim couldn't possibly be true.

The opening paragraph continues, "This is because not very many happy things happened in the lives of the three Baudelaire youngsters [our protagonists].... They were charming, and resourceful, and had pleasant facial features." That sounds like we could stomach meeting this trio. And facially, they don't look like mutant monsters. I suppose that's a plus.

Then the author gets right back to his initial premise: "Everything that happened to them was rife with misfortune, misery, and despair. I'm sorry to tell you this, but that is how the story goes." It's a more-than-intriguing beginning from someone who has chosen to write under the name *Lemony Snicket*, which sounds like a cookie treat made with nothing but lemon and sunshine. But the author is trying to sell us on the notion that *nothing* good happens in his story. Seemingly, the only choice appears to be to read the book and find out. Genius!

ALMOST NEVER

"All children, except one, grow up." That's the iconic opening line to Scottish novelist J. M. Barrie's *Peter and Wendy* (1911). And naturally, the boy to whom Barrie is referring is Peter Pan, resident of Neverland, leader of the Lost Boys, friend of the fairy Tinker Bell, and archenemy of the pirate Captain Hook. You've probably met the character in dozens of different incarnations—movies, TV shows, cartoons, and other vehicles that draw on Barrie's work as inspiration.

Why is Barrie's opening line so memorable and telling? It instantly captures our attention and imagination—the thought of accessing the Fountain of Youth. But it is also quite the paradox of contrasting ideas. Growing up is something done by everyone. How could it be different just for Peter?

Wendy, the other young adult protagonist in the title, has no such power to delay the inevitable. In the opening paragraph, Wendy, as a two-year-old, picks a flower for her mother, who wishes her daughter could remain that age forever. But Barrie instantly informs us, "You always know after you are two. Two is the beginning of the end."

As we get to know Peter through the story, we may not want to be exactly like him. Yes, he's adventurous, brave, and all about fun, but he's also childish, self-centered, and narcissistic. And why not? He's never grown up—still has all his baby teeth, according to Barrie.

After some time in Neverland, Wendy, along with her two younger siblings and even Peter's tribe, the Lost Boys, decides it's time to go home and grow up. So Barrie's opening line actually holds true: Peter stands alone, with no desire to move forward. (Tinker Bell is a fairy; she doesn't need to grow up.)

Psychologists have also tapped into Barrie's never-maturing character. The term for men who find it difficult to grow up and maintain adult relationships is wonderfully called Peter Pan syndrome.

> *If you could go back to being a little kid for an entire weekend, what would you want to do? Do you think there's anything you would miss about being older over those two days?*

MISSING PARENTS

Appropriately, Peter is an orphan, with no role model of maturity in his life. Many literary characters are orphans, enabling the writer to give these characters different outside influences and to place them in situations from which most parents would undoubtedly attempt to protect them. These orphans include Batman, Harry Potter, Oliver Twist, Tarzan, Cinderella, Jane Eyre, James Bond, Lilo (from *Lilo and Stitch*) and Little Orphan Annie.

ANGST PERSONIFIED

Holden Caulfield (age sixteen) is a student at boarding prep school. Well, at least he used to be. That was before Holden got expelled for failing all his classes, except English. That's a good thing for us—Holden having passable communication skills—because he's the narrator of a novel by J. D. Salinger, *The Catcher in the Rye* (1951). Holden has long been a poster child (poster teen, actually) for adolescent rebellion.

Here is Salinger's rambling opening line for his protagonist: "If you really want to hear about it, the first thing you'll probably want to know is where I was born, and what my lousy childhood was like, and how my parents were occupied and all before they had me, and all that David Copperfield kind of crap, but I don't feel like going into it, if you want to know the truth." I know, it's a run-on sentence. Let's get past that. It's actually a spot-on beginning, providing a self-described reluctant storyteller who is actually in the process of telling us his story. That's a cool concept. And we absolutely do "want to know the truth" from Holden. Or else what's the point?

There's also the allusion to David Copperfield (not the magician), who is the lead character in the Charles Dickens novel *David Copperfield* (1850), detailing his rather bleak childhood during Victorian times and journey to maturity. Holden's rebellion? He doesn't tell his parents that he's been expelled and instead goes on a trip to New York City for several days, trying in part to stretch his wings and live like an adult—something for which Holden Caulfield is really not prepared.

What about the title, *The Catcher in the Rye*? Holden envisions himself being the guardian of children who are playing in a tall field of rye, with the perilous drop off a steep cliff hidden from their view. He makes sure they never unwittingly go over the edge, perhaps like he's symbolically done himself.

THE ANTI-HOLDEN (SAVE FERRIS!)

The scheming and manipulative high schooler Ferris Bueller, the protagonist of the cult-classic teen film *Ferris Bueller's Day Off* (1986), simply wants one thing in life: not to go to school today. Why? Because the weather's too nice outside.

"How could I possibly be expected to handle school on a day like this?" says Ferris, who needs to outwit his parents by playing sick. And haven't we all been there!

Screenwriter John Hughes opens the film with Ferris lying in bed, moaning, as his concerned parents look on. "He doesn't have a fever, but he says his stomach hurts, and he's seeing spots," Ferris's mom informs his dad.

Ferris protests the thought of his parents keeping him at home: "I'm fine. I have a test today. I have to take it."

That's when his older sister comes in and can see straight through Ferris's act. "Yeah, right. Dry that one out, and you can fertilize the lawn with it," says Jeanie, whose teen eyes are sharper than her parents' judgment at this moment.

As soon as his parents are gone to work, Ferris rises out of bed, stares directly into the camera, breaking down the fourth wall separating the characters from the audience, and informs us, "Incredible. One of the worst performances of my career, and they never doubted it for a second."

It's a superb opening by Hughes because the audience, who understood all along that Ferris was faking, gets taken into the protagonist's confidence while understanding that Jeanie, who's totally jealous of the brother's ability to hoodwink their parents, is willing to be a problem in Ferris's larger plans for the day.

What are Ferris's plans? Simply to enjoy himself to the max, exploring nearly every inch of his hometown, Chicago, along with a pair of friends whom he also helps spring from school. His fellow classmates, believing he's really sick, even start a Save Ferris fundraiser. Everyone finds Ferris easy to root for—except Jeanie.

MODELED UPON

The power of parody is on full display in the opening scene of *Captain Underpants: The First Epic Movie* (2017). Narrating for the audience are the fourth-grade creators of the title character, George Beard and

Harold Hutchins (the actual author and illustrator of the graphic novel series is Dav Pilkey). The kids begin, "A long, long, long, long time ago in a galaxy far, far away, there was a planet called Underpanty World."

That's how to channel your inner *Star Wars*! Only the grade schoolers aren't finished borrowing from their favorite storylines. You see, the peaceful Underpanty World is about to blow up, so the ruling parents—Big Daddy Long Johns and Princess Pantyhose—shoot their infant son into space (via the elastic in his underpants waistband), and he lands in a farm field on Earth.

Does this sound familiar, fans of Superman? But just as you think the Kent family is going to rescue and adopt the infant, who possesses superhuman strength, instead it's a pair of land-bound, farmer dolphins. No, I'm not kidding. "Just go with it," our narrators urge us.

Why is it such a perfectly penned opening? Fourth graders who draw their own comics (in this case George and Harold co-own Tree House Comix, Inc.) are normally inspired by a myriad of comics, movies, TV shows, books, and music they adore. So borrowing a few ideas from those vehicles while adding a new spin of their own is right on target.

What about Captain Underpants? He's really the school principal, Mr. Krupp, who's a meanie on the surface but turns into Captain Underpants after being hypnotized by George and Harold. It seems Principal Krupp is an undercover fan of the homemade comics he confiscates from the pair of burgeoning writers/illustrators. Krupp isn't all bad, just misunderstood, like so many adults.

> Search your memory. What's the first story you ever sat down to write or illustrate? Was it an assignment for school or rather something you did just for pleasure?

HARRY IS STILL HARRY

It's ironic the way life hasn't imitated art in the case of British author J. K. Rowling and her novel *Harry Potter and the Philosopher's Stone* (1997), the first in the series of Harry Potter books, which is responsible for creating a generation of literature lovers. The opening line of the novel reads, "Mr. and Mrs. Dursley of number four, Privet Drive, were proud to say that they were perfectly normal, thank you very much." This is a clear path to Rowling's characterization of Harry's pursuit of acceptance in a world that has basically rejected him.

With the "Thank you, very much" there for emphasis, the Dursleys, a Muggle, or nonmagic, family and the only living relatives of Harry after the murder of his parents by the infamous Lord Voldemort, have clearly ostracized him for being different. One of the main themes explored by Rowling is Harry's quest to find a place where he belongs, with people who accept him regardless of his birthright and despite the lightning-bolt scar on his forehead, which differentiates him from the other wizards. This is clearly a heavy burden for an eleven-year-old.

That's why the transphobic statements made by Rowling in 2023 offend people so deeply; she had written a novel about acceptance that permeated our culture. Readers expected her to be that same person in her societal views. But literature and real life don't always perfectly align. Still, Harry Potter is Harry Potter with no deviation. And in Rowling's literary hands, readers worldwide embrace a character who is portrayed as anything but "perfectly normal."

NOT SO WIMPY

Diary of a Wimpy Kid (2007) is billed as a novel in cartoons. And the drawings of author/illustrator Jeff Kinney are hugely important to the multibook series, giving the reader a visual for middle school protagonist Greg Heffley, the band of characters in his close orbit, and some hilarious comic relief. But Kinney's writing is near flawless in representing the perspective of middle schoolers.

Here's Greg Heffley's personal introduction to us in the opening lines of the series: "First of all, let me get something straight: This is a JOURNAL, not a diary. I know what it says on the cover, but when Mom went out to buy this thing I SPECIFICALLY told her to get one that didn't say 'diary' on it.... All I need is for some jerk to catch me carrying this book around and get the wrong idea."

There's little doubt that Greg believes diaries are for girls, that boys can at least be seen making an entry in a journal without their budding manhood being challenged by some testosterone-driven bully. Need proof? Notice how *JOURNAL* is written in all capitals, along with *SPECIFICALLY*—his request that his mom comes back with a book that doesn't say "diary" on it. But to our total amusement and Greg's dismay, that didn't happen.

The possible social and physical consequences are very real to Greg: "Let me just say for the record that I think middle school is the dumbest idea ever invented. You got kids like me who haven't hit their growth spurt yet mixed in with these gorillas who need to shave twice a day." The author's opening lines give us a keen glimpse into Greg's middle school universe. And we start to root for Greg from his first words because he's brave enough to write in a diary and willing to trust us with his most personal thoughts in its pages.

ALWAYS ONLINE

Ever get annoyed that your phone and computer seem to show you ads about things you've mentioned in recent conversations? That's almost nothing compared to the near-future world envisioned by author T. M. Anderson in his young adult novel *Feed* (2002), where most people have a feed (supplying Feednet, an outgrowth of the internet) wired directly into their brains since the time they were infants.

How powerful can this 24/7 conscious and subliminal consumerism be, especially beneath a sky where even the clouds have sponsored ads? Here's Anderson's opening line to the novel: "We went to the moon to have fun, but the moon turned out to completely suck."

Imagine being maneuvered into going clubbing on the moon (it's really gone downhill since Neil Armstrong walked there and is now treated like a dumping ground for old trash) for spring break because your feed convinced you it's where the *teenage in-crowd* is headed.

It's an opening line that simultaneously shocks and intrigues the audience, juxtaposing the ideas that a trip to the moon, which on the surface seems fantastically exciting, could actually "suck."

Don't worry. Not every teen in this society believes in the feed, and somebody hacks into it.

> *How do you feel about commercials? Do they add (pun intended) anything to your life, or are they just a waste of your time? How might you change where, when, and how many commercials we see in our society?*

PIT STOP 2

*Reflecting on What We've Seen and
What's to Come and More Potential Projects*

Alright, we've traveled approximately two-thirds of this literary journey exploring perfectly penned opening lines, and we're making the final turn into the homestretch. By the way, that's a racing metaphor (car, foot, horse, ostrich—yes, they race ostriches). But remember, literature isn't a competition, and there's no real finish line. You can start and stop whenever you please. The only real goal is to enjoy yourself, whether you're reading, writing, or outlining something that you eventually want to create.

Perhaps you've been inspired to write a sleuth story, featuring your own preteen or teen detective or create your own super and pen their short introduction to the world, describing who they are? Or maybe like the character Kat Stratford from the film *10 Things I Hate about You*, you want to construct your own fourteen-line sonnet telling about your relationship with someone (please don't *hate* them).

The possibilities are really endless. It's all about your motivation and imagination. I know you can do it, so get ready to sail (I'm mixing metaphors, I get it) through the final chapters and experience a piece of work that hopefully becomes one of your *new* favorites.

THIRTEEN
THE SENSES AND UNITY AND DISCORD

THE SENSES

Writers of all genres love to engage our five senses: sight, hearing, smell, taste, and touch. It can become an incredibly interactive journey, with the audience physically experiencing the writer's words and images. But it takes a special piece of material to evoke that kind of reaction. With that in mind, I've chosen several works to present, each with a focus on one or more of the five senses and containing perfectly penned opening lines to facilitate such a feeling connection.

ALPHABET SOUP

Lots of readers claim that they have a ravenous appetite and basically devour several books a week. Only they don't really eat those books, do they? Here's a piece from Canadian-born Mark Strand, a Pulitzer Prize–winning poet who also harbored a love for painting, challenging the idea of how to *devour* literature with his ultrasurreal "Eating Poetry" (2014). Strand's opening lines leave nothing and everything to the imagination:

> Ink runs from the corners of my mouth.
> There is no happiness like mine.
> I have been eating poetry.

The perfect metaphor is sealed with the image of the ink, which moments ago had been married to pages, running from the corners of the speaker's mouth. He also boasts to us that his happiness is unique and, in a sense, more powerful than ours could ever be with a piece of poetry. Or maybe at this point, we should call it a *slice*.

Strand isn't backing off from this concept of literally eating a poem:

> The librarian does not believe what she sees.

Who wouldn't smile at watching the librarian, man or woman, freak out at the notion of someone actually gnawing on a book?

So what's the poem that the speaker is eating about? Strand doesn't specifically tell us, but dogs are now on the library's basement stairs, ascending upward. And suddenly, our speaker starts to do some very canine-like things:

> I snarl at her and bark.
> I romp with joy in the bookish dark.

That's the type of sense-filled journey a writer like Mark Strand can establish with an opening line that so artfully awakens our poetic palate.

> *What do you imagine literature tastes like? Would short stories taste differently than poems or plays? Or would the taste of art vary by subject matter? Can you compare the imagined taste of the last book you read to that of a particular food?*

SPEAKING UP

Singer/songwriter Paul Simon penned a sense-filled song, "The Sound of Silence" (1964), that became a counterculture anthem of the 1960s, challenging listeners to think and ultimately take part in shaping the type of society in which they want to live. The piece immerses the audience in the senses of sight and sound, celebrating them by warning of their potential loss if people choose to sit idly by and not participate, most notably through their silence.

Simon's superb opening line brings the listener into a world with the possibility of going dim:

> Hello, darkness, my old friend
> I've come to talk with you again

Paul Simon personifies darkness, turning it into something alive, something with which we can hold a conversation. But the opening also suggests that we've become too comfortable with our diminishing light and sound. Will the world be drowned out in a deafening and darkened silence? Out of fear? Out of passiveness? And what about songwriters like Paul Simon?

His speaker laments of

> people writing songs that voices never shared
> And no one dared
> Disturb the sound of silence

But Simon's speaker won't be among those remaining mute. There's just too much at stake. And don't forget, he's singing to us at the moment, standing by his beliefs:

> "Fools" said I, "You do not know
> Silence like a cancer grows."

Paul Simon's personification of darkness and silence paints them as powerful foes, providing "The Sound of Silence" with a chilling urgency. Go give it a listen!

DEEP BREATHS

An American poet and practicing physician of Latin descent, William Carlos Williams takes on one of the lesser-explored senses in his odoriferous poem "Smell!" (1917). His opening line establishes direct communication with his nose, scolding it for smelling anything it so pleases:

> Oh strong-ridged and deeply hollowed
> nose of mine! what will you not be smelling?

It's as if his nose has a *mind* of its own, and that's supremely interesting. Williams describes his nostrils as

> always indiscriminate, always unashamed

Rank. Rotting. Putrid. Noisome. Reeking. Malodorous. Rancid. Moldy. Stinky. Foul. Apparently Williams has little control over his adventurous olfactory sense. And the seemingly powerless poet is pleading for a change:

> Can you not be decent? Can you not reserve your ardors
> for something less unlovely?

How about a rose bush or freshly baked cinnamon roll instead of a wheelbarrow full of fertilizer?

> Must you taste everything? Must you know everything?
> Must you have a part in everything?

The sweet scent of achievement here is that the poet has established that he is fighting a losing battle with his free-spirited nose, something that he deftly establishes in the opening line for us to take forward.

BEYOND US

Australian poet and environmentalist Judith Wright (1915–2000) penned "Five Senses" (1963), a poem that binds the senses together into a singular, mystical force with the ability to create phenomenal moments and feelings, seemingly out of nothing:

> Now my five senses
> gather into a meaning
> all acts, all presences

The opening line describes the senses as operating outside her control. And that's part of the beautiful mystery. When is that happening?

"Now." It's a time marker that gives the poem a striking immediacy every time it's read.

Wright (who is wonderfully our *writer*) compares the cohesiveness of her senses to a flower or a weaver fashioning together textures and fragrances, spinning a delicate thread, or webbing into something totally new—a one-of-a-kind experience just for her:

> While I'm in my five senses
> they send me spinning
> all sounds and silences,
> all shape and colour

No need to be jealous. This could be you, too. Just open your mind—I mean, your senses. For Wright, this sense creation is a sublime act that she doesn't truly comprehend. *Hmm.* Our senses operating on a level beyond our sensibilities. That's a true sense of wonder.

Wright's closing line beautifully mirrors her spot-on opening, which set this sense stage for us:

> some pattern sprung from nothing—
> a rhythm that dances
> and is not mine.

YOU FILL UP MY SENSES

Can immersing your senses in the great outdoors influence your writing? It did for singer/songwriter John Denver, who penned "Annie's Song" (1974) in less than ten minutes while on a chairlift to the top of Aspen Mountain in Colorado, after just completing a difficult and exhausting ski run. The song begins,

> You fill up my senses like a night in a forest,
> like the mountains in springtime, like a walk in the rain

The string of similes instantly connects the listener to their own recollections of such instances because Denver doesn't supply any specific details for us.

The opening stanza beautifully continues in the same detail-less manner, with adjectives providing a hint of color to which our own memories can begin to shade:

> like a storm in the desert, like a sleepy blue ocean.
> You fill up my senses, come fill me again.

Who's Annie from the title? She was Denver's wife at the time, but Annie is never mentioned by name in the song, giving the listener the opportunity to envision their own loved one as the lyrical inspiration.

> *How many songs can you name in which the title of the song doesn't appear in the lyrics? These songs are few and far between, but they're out there.*

UNITY AND DISCORD

Often it feels as if the world revolves around the opposing forces of unity and discord. Are we all together on an idea or solution to a current problem? Or are we so entrenched in our different views that we can't make an inch of progress through open dialogue and negotiation? Writers have long been drawn to the celebration of unity and the drama of discord as themes for their work. Why? There is normally intense passion to be explored in both extremes.

LOVE LIGHT

Hafiz was a Persian mystical poet in the fourteenth century. He penned an incredible short poem, or ghazel, of cosmic unity through the personification of the Sun and our Earth, describing them in an intimate relationship. The translation of his opening line reads,

> Even
> After
> All this time
> The Sun never says to the Earth,
>
> "You owe me."

Despite writing that opening more than six centuries ago, the phrase *Even after all this time* is an apt description. Incredibly, the Sun and Earth have existed together for some 4.6 billion years, making the 600 years separating Hafiz and us seem like just a few fleeting seconds.

Hafiz gives the Sun the ability to speak, and therefore the Earth has the ability to at least listen, maybe even answer back. And all we know about that is what the Sun *doesn't say*: requesting a thank-you. That's a startling beginning, opening the audience's mind to a myriad of conversational possibilities or periods of prolonged silence between the two heavenly bodies.

And what is it about the relationship between the pair? Just as we begin to wonder, Hafiz finishes his piece with a brushstroke of unity and bliss:

Look
What happens
With a love like that,
It lights the whole sky.

> If the Earth and Sun could actually have a conversation, what do you think they would talk about? Would they ever argue, compliment one another, or perhaps even tell a joke?

THE PRICE AND REWARD

It's no secret that artists spend many solitary hours planning, writing, and then (more often than not) rewriting their work until it shines the way they had envisioned. Those hours could be spent sitting alone in front of the blue light of a computer screen and keyboard, but they can also be spent in the midst of friends and family, with the artist's thoughts focused on their work instead of the conversation at hand. So if you know a writer in the middle of producing a piece, don't be offended if it appears they're not listening to you.

Poet Rose Marie Juan-austin has wonderfully balanced the price of an artist's hours alone with the rewards of creation in "Poetry Is a Solitary Art" (2018). She begins with the opening lines,

> Poetry is a solitary art
> But beautiful words come alive
> While we write.

Here the speaker/poet has the ability to actually breathe life into words. It's a mixture of hyperbole and personification to the highest degree, all taking place in a universe that rises and falls via a snap of the artist's fingers:

> As we go on penning
> ...words...
> Laugh and dance
> ...touch our hearts

In Juan-austin's hands, the verb *go penning* feels like an absolute pleasure and triumph, without a second's regret over the time it might have taken—time not lost but somehow gained anew. It's a marvelous poetic experience for anyone who has ever labored over the correct order of what others might consider several meaningless words.

> *Have you ever experienced writer's block, grasping for just the right word or image to complete a piece of artistic work or school assignment? What are your personal solutions for getting your mind to clear and refocus?*

SHARING THE LOAD

Bill Withers, a native of Stab Fork, West Virginia, overcame a stuttering problem as a youth to take his place among the finest singer/songwriters of the twentieth century. His ability to communicate loneliness, sorrow, and heartbreak through both his lyrics and soulful voice earned him worldwide acclaim. But being a superstar didn't particularly interest Bill Withers, who walked away from the music industry and his thriving career in the mid-1980s. "I feel that it is healthier to look out at the world through a window than through a mirror. Otherwise, all you see is yourself and whatever is behind you," said Withers concerning his outlook on life.[1]

When Withers moved to Los Angeles, he missed the community of the small coal-mining town in which he grew up, so he penned the song "Lean on Me" (1972) as a lyrical bridge connecting a lone voice to a vast amount of others. Withers's opening line instantly binds the audience in a shared experience:

> Sometimes in our lives, we all have pain
> We all have sorrow

But the speaker, knowing how hard life can be, isn't going to turn his back on anyone:

> Lean on me when you're not strong
> And I'll be your friend
> I'll help you carry on

Withers understands that what goes around comes around and that hard times could be just around the corner in the speaker's life, as well:

> For it won't be long
> 'Til I'm gonna need
> Somebody to lean on

It's a song that completes a unifying circle—*I'll be there for you and you'll be there for me*—all begun with an opening line to which everyone can relate on a heartfelt level.

ISLAND OR CONTINENT

John Donne was an English poet, scholar, and soldier whose life spanned the late sixteenth century to almost the mid-seventeenth century. Donne is best known for penning the line "No man is an island," and the several lines that follow. You might be under the belief that it's a poem, but it's an excerpt from a larger prose work, *Devotions upon Emergent Occasions* (1624). The excerpt begins, "No man is an island, entire of itself, every man is a piece of the continent, a part of the main." It's a terrific metaphor, equating people to land masses—the limited shore of an island to the immensity of a continent.

Donne, who wrote this after a near-death experience with a serious and mysterious illness, is conveying that there is strength in unified numbers, that humankind is better off as an infinite connection than as a small series of selfish or individual souls. "Any man's death diminishes me," Donne continues.

It's not often that a work produces a pair of famous lines, especially within the space of just a handful of sentences, but the excerpt's final line has certainly made an impact of its own: "Therefore never send to know for whom the bell tolls; it tolls for thee." The bell is most likely a church bell ringing at a funeral.

The notion that anyone's death means a small piece of *you* dies, as well, comes back full circle to the powerful opening, "No man is an island entire of itself."

CLOSING THE CIRCLE

The comedy series *Seinfeld*, created by Jerry Seinfeld and Larry David, ran on NBC for nine seasons (1989–1998). That was before streaming, so it was considered "appointment television," meaning you had to be at home in front of your TV on the night and time it actually aired if you wanted to see it. And during the final several seasons, people did, in droves. An estimated 76.3 million viewers tuned in for the final episode.

The show's scripts launched a number of phrases into our lexicon. They include being a *close talker* (someone who stands almost on top of you as they speak); the *double dip* (putting a chip back into the dip bowl after taking a bite out of it); *regifting* (taking an unwanted gift and giving it to someone else); and *yada, yada, yada* (used as a filler in conversation to avoid telling the real details). But despite these popular phrases, the series opened and closed with basically the exact same nondescript line about the placement of the second button (from the top down) on a button-down shirt.

Sitting in a coffee shop at the start of the first episode, Jerry tells his best friend George, "You see to me that button is in the worst possible spot. The second button literally makes or breaks the shirt." It's an almost insignificant line that has nothing to do with the soon-to-be-unfolding plot. Only the line does hint that the show is going to be, in part, about observations and the characters' daily lives. In other words, it would be *a show about nothing*.

Nine seasons later, with the pair now sitting in a jail cell and contemplating a one-year sentence behind bars for breaking the Good Samaritan Law—making fun of a robbery victim instead of trying to help him (no, we're not kidding)—Jerry again comments to George about that button: "The second button is the key button. It literally makes or breaks the shirt. Look at it. It's too high."

To which the pair seem to have a moment of recognition and déjà vu. "Didn't we have this conversation before?" asks George as the scene fades out.

What's the point of replaying that seemingly meaningless line? It's all about the unification of a circle that began in episode 1 and closed in episode 180. Coming full circle, especially in comedy writing, is a connective technique known as the callback, which rings a satisfying bell in the audience's memory.

FOURTEEN
FANTASY

The genre of fantasy often takes place in an imaginary universe. The normal physical rules that govern our everyday existence, such as gravity, biology, and the laws of matter and energy, can either be suspended or rearranged to fit the artist's vision. Aliens or fictional humanoid races, like vampires, fairies, elves, giants, dwarves, and magical beings, often hold dominion. But no matter the artist's otherworldly vision, the most celebrated fantasy novels, films, short stories, and plays maintain a visible reflection of *our* world and society. Why? It's rather simple. An audience comprised of human beings, not a super race of highly evolved squirrels, needs to connect to the storyline. To make that possible, even when a story is set in an alternative universe, artists will focus on themes important to us, including love, hope, conflict, and betrayal. And, of course, that connection starts with the artist's opening lines.

So the next time you find yourself thoroughly engrossed in fantasy, pause for a moment and ask yourself, "What connects this story to the human condition?" I guarantee that connection to our daily lives will be there.

SNEAK PEAK

When your story revolves around vampires—those bloodsucking, undead, mythical creatures that find their origin in European folklore—then death is going to usually be in the air. Stephenie Meyer, author of the young adult vampire romance series *Twilight*, understands this completely—so much so that her first book in the series, *Twilight* (2005), begins with a preface of a scene pulled from the body of the work, giving readers a glance at what's to come. An unnamed narrator begins, "I'd never given much thought to how I would die—though I'd had reason enough in the last few months—but even if I had, I would not have imagined it like this. I stared without breathing across the long room, into the dark eyes of the hunter, and he looked pleasantly back at me." It's a perfect bull's-eye of a beginning because as the book starts to unfold before us, we try to identify those characters, both the narrator and the hunter. And when we're sure that we have it right, as readers we're very satisfied with ourselves.

In the opening chapter, we're introduced to our narrator, Bella Swan, who's moving from the blue-skied desert city of Phoenix, known as the Valley of the Sun, to the town of Forks, Washington, in the Pacific Northwest. "Forks existed under near-constant cover of clouds. It rains on this inconsequential town more than any other place in the United States of America," notes Bella.

Cloud cover? *Hmm*, don't vampires hate the sunlight? In *Forks*? Meyer is discretely setting the table for us (and the undead) through her delectable use of images. Bon appétit!

TOLL TAKER

Brooklyn-born author Norton Juster penned the fantasy classic *The Phantom Tollbooth* (1961). The protagonist is ten-year-old Milo, who is bored with everything in the world—not just kind of bored but bored beyond the limits of boredom. The youngster's first phrase? "It seems to me that almost everything is a waste of time." A bit of exaggeration? Perhaps. But the hyperbolic thought that Milo is *never* interested in *anything* helps to really establish his character.

Here's the novel's opening lines, which similarly drive home the author's point: "There was once a boy named Milo who didn't know what to do with himself—not just sometimes, but always. When he was in school he longed to be out, and when he was out he longed to be in. On the way he thought about coming home, and coming home he thought about going." Now that's a kid without a focus!

But when Milo arrives home, there's a mysterious gift awaiting him. The package reads, "One Genuine Turnpike Tollbooth." The included magical map provides Milo with unheard-of destinations and even gives the guarantee "If not perfectly satisfied, your wasted time will be refunded." Suddenly, Milo is off on an adventure, along with Tock, a watchdog—with a clock in its stomach—that can sniff out wasted time, and the Humbug, a bug-like traveler with a nasty attitude.

Will Milo be more interested in the world by actually *doing* instead of learning about it in school through memorizing and reciting facts? Feel free to decide for yourself because the pages of Juster's *The Phantom Tollbooth* are still open to connoisseurs of boredom—I mean readers just like you.

> *If you could have just one magical coin to toss into the Phantom Tollbooth and could go anywhere in the universe, to a place real or imagined, where would you choose to travel?*

STORM ON THE HORIZON

Sometimes stories evolve right out of a writer's life. Author Rick Riordan's son Haley is dyslexic, affecting his ability to read and spell. While studying mythology with his second-grade class, Haley asked his dad to tell him bedtime stories using the same characters. Eventually, the author began including his own fictitious characters in the mythical landscape. That led to the creation of Percy Jackson, a half-blood and demigod, as the son of Poseidon and a mortal woman. Here's Riordan's opening lines from the first in the Percy Jackson and the Olympians series, *The Lightning Thief* (2005): "Look, I didn't want to be a half-blood. If you're reading this because you think you might be one, my advice is: close the book right now. Believe whatever lie your mom or dad told you about your birth, and try to lead a normal life."

It's an eye-opening beginning, with Percy citing the danger and despair in his life, even before the first turn of the page. *Please, you don't want to be like me. Just go back to your life*, is the type of start that instantly focuses an audience and gains their attention. Because deep down, Riordan realizes you want to take that adventure.

What was stolen by the Lightning Thief? Zeus's master bolt, the weapon on which all other lightning bolts are fashioned. As I've mentioned previously in discussing fantasy, comparing imaginary universes to our own world gives the audience a great point of reference on which to draw emotions. And Riordan is a master of making those fantasy-reality connections, as pilfering that master bolt would be the equivalent of stealing several nuclear warheads in our society.

RABBIT HOLE

Some of literature's best-known characters are Alice, the White Rabbit, the grinning Cheshire Cat, and the Queen of Hearts from Lewis Carroll's novel *Alice's Adventures in Wonderland* (1865). How did these fantasy characters spring from Carroll's imagination? The author was rowing a small boat along an English river. Among the passengers were the children of a friend, and one of them was named Alice. Carroll passed the time on the journey by telling the children stories. Later, Alice requested that the author make her a copy of one particular tale featuring a girl her age with the same name.

Here's how Carroll starts his story: "Alice was beginning to get very tired of sitting by her sister on the [river] bank, and of having nothing to do: once or twice she had peeped into the book her sister was reading, but it had no pictures or conversations in it, 'and what is the use of a book,' thought Alice 'without pictures or conversation?'"

Naturally, *Alice's Adventures in Wonderland* contains both dialogue and illustrations. That will stop a book from being boring! In a sense, through his own opening line, Carroll writes a positive review and commercial on why you should continue. Ingenious!

All of a sudden, Alice sees a white rabbit in a waistcoat scurrying along, speaking to itself, saying, "Oh dear! I shall be late!" Then the rabbit quickly checks its watch. A talking rabbit in a waistcoat, carrying a pocket watch? "Alice started to her feet . . . burning with curiosity, she ran across the field after it, and fortunately was just in time to see it pop down a large rabbit-hole under the hedge." Alice follows the rabbit down the hole, falling and tumbling into Wonderland.

That scene gets put into motion by Carroll's brilliant opening lines of a young girl who thought her sister's book to be boring, so she found an adventure of her own. Good going, Alice! And a much-deserved thanks to both the fictional and real Alice for requesting this story be written down.

> ### ALLUSIONS TO ALICE
>
> Grace Slick wrote and performed the song "White Rabbit" (1967) with the San Francisco–based rock band Jefferson Airplane. It debuted in the late 1960s, when psychedelic drugs were emerging into mainstream America. In her song, Slick alludes to scenes throughout *Alice's Adventures in Wonderland*, in which Alice and other characters ingest various substances that seem to contribute to their fantastical view of Wonderland. Slick's lyrics begin
>
> > One pill makes you larger
> > And one pill makes you small . . .
> > Go ask Alice
> > When she's ten feet tall.
>
> There is no mention of personal drug use in Carroll's diaries, though drugs were readily available, and many were not illegal in nineteenth-century Great Britain. But Grace Slick wasn't the first to make the connection between psychedelics and Carroll's novels. As a result, many US school districts banned *Alice's Adventures in Wonderland* during different eras, believing it somehow promoted the use of drugs.

BUTTERCUP AND WESTLEY

You're probably familiar with *The Princess Bride* (1987). It's a romance/fantasy film based on a novel with perhaps the longest title you have ever witnessed jammed onto a book cover: *The Princess Bride: S. Morgenstern's Classic Tale of True Love and High Adventure, The "Good Parts" Version* (1973). Now you know why the title was reduced for the movie. They never would have been able to fit the original onto a theater marquee. William Goldman was both the author of the novel and the screenwriter of the film, and he gave audiences two incredible but very different openings to advance the stories forward.

The Princess Bride is Buttercup, and the book begins by examining the life of the most beautiful woman in the world at different intervals in Buttercup's young life: "The year that Buttercup was born, the most beautiful woman in the world was a French scullery maid named Annette. Annette worked in Paris for the Duke and Duchess de Guiche, and it did not escape the Duke's notice that someone extraordinary was polishing the pewter."

I know, you think the Duke's wife, the Duchess, had Annette immediately fired or possibly even beheaded. No, something much better. The Duchess discovers Annette's weakness is chocolate and feeds her enough of it to pack on fifty pounds or so, proving that the Duke was only attracted to her petite figure. The opening lines suggest that great beauty is a double-edged sword. Some people will admire you solely for that single attribute, and others will be entirely jealous. Either camp may not have your best interests at heart.

It turns out that Buttercup's true love is a farmhand named Westley, who is too poor to marry her. So he goes off to seek his fortune, but is presumed killed at the hands of desperate pirates. Don't worry. Westley talks his way out of danger, befriending the pirates and learning how to fight.

Buttercup wasn't born a princess, but with Westley believed dead, she eventually agrees to marry a prince who simply wants to possess Buttercup for her beauty—that double-edged sword the author put forth in the opening lines. Well played, William Goldman.

How does Goldman choose to begin his film version? A young boy is stuck at home, sick in bed, when his grandfather comes to visit. "I brought you a special present," says the grandfather.

After unwrapping it, the boy is less than thrilled to see that it's a book. The grandfather explains, "It's the book my father used to read to me when I was sick, and I used to read it to your father. And today I'm going to read it to you." The continuation of the tradition certainly feels important, and the audience is invited to share in the moment, as if they were family, too.

Still unconvinced, the boy wants to know if the book is exciting. The grandfather exclaims that it has "fencing, fighting, torture, revenge, giants, monsters, chases, escapes, true love and miracles!" It's a book talk that any librarian would have traded their oversized reading glasses (dangling from a beaded chain around their neck) to make! Naturally, that book is the story of Westley and Buttercup's adventurous romance.

Two marvelous beginnings—one phenomenal story.

HOBBITS AND RINGS

John Ronald Reuel Tolkien (1892–1973), an English novelist and writer of fantasy, is more widely known by his first three initials: J. R. R. It can easily be argued that the genre of fantasy was still very much considered a second-rate form of literary expression until Tolkien published a pair of iconic novels that elevated its artistic ceiling and popularity.

In 1937, Tolkien began *The Hobbit* with these lines: "In a hole in the ground there lived a hobbit. Not a nasty, dirty, wet hole, filled with the ends of worms and an oozy smell, nor yet a dry, bare, sandy hole with nothing in it to sit down on or to eat: it was a hobbit hole, and that means comfort." We now have a starting point, a toe in the ground, if you will, to begin deciphering this world and part of its inhabitants.

So what's a hobbit? Mainly farmers and gardeners, hobbits are a race resembling humans, except that they're rather short with furry, leathery feet—which seems appropriate because Tolkien lets us know immediately that they prefer living underground.

Our protagonist is a hobbit named Bilbo Baggins, and he is absolutely a creature of comfort. His hole has paneled walls, tiled and carpeted floors, fancy furniture, and rooms filled with wardrobes of fashionable clothing. Part of the reason Bilbo is such a respected hobbit is because of his predictability; hobbits, almost as a rule, live very established and quiet lives. Only Tolkien fully understands that wouldn't make much of a fantasy tale, so we encounter Baggins on the cusp of a huge change.

Bilbo Baggins is about to be tricked into aligning himself with a famous wizard; joining forces with a band of warrior-like dwarves; and trying to reclaim a vast, stolen fortune from a fire-breathing dragon standing guard over it; "This is a story of how a Baggins had an adventure, found himself doing and saying things altogether unexpected. He may have lost the neighbors' respect, but he gained well, you will see whether he gained anything in the end."

In a fantastical world that he's in the midst of establishing, Tolkien gives us a glimpse of routine Middle-earth and then turns that landscape upside down by sending Bilbo Baggins on what would be the quest of any hobbit's life. "As we all know, ultimately, we've only got humanity to work with. It's the only clay we've got. In the end, of course, any races you make, if they're speaking and thinking, are taking certain parts of humanity as one knows it. Slight alterations and emphasis, that's all you can do, isn't it?" Tolkien commented in a 1965 interview on creating the inhabitants of Middle-earth.[1]

With fans of fantasy around the globe clamoring for a sequel to *The Hobbit*, Tolkien put in more than a decade of writing and revising before he published *The Lord of the Rings* (1954). Tolkien's opening lines again focus on Bilbo Baggins, who is the current keeper of the One Ring created by the Dark Lord, which has the ability to rule the other rings of power and possibly conquer Middle-earth.

The novel explains, "When Mr. Bilbo Baggins of Bag End announced that he would shortly be celebrating his eleventy-first birthday with a party of special magnificence, there was much talk and excitement in Hobbiton." "Eleventy-first"? That's pretty old. Too old for the next quest? Another hobbit in the wings waiting to emerge a hero?

Bilbo seems to have both eternal youth and riches beyond compare. But hobbits are very practical about such matters, believing that no such *good fortune* comes without paying an appropriate price. Bilbo's neighbors remark, "It will have to be paid for.... It isn't natural, and trouble will come of it!"

That price tag, along with the One Ring (the undeniable cause of Bilbo barely aging) is inherited by Frodo Baggins (a much younger cousin), who comes to understand that the One Ring must be destroyed at all costs by sending it down the Crack of Doom, a deep chasm filled with fire where the ring was originally forged. It is another daunting quest for a hobbit who has so far led a quiet life, put in motion by the opening line.

Of Frodo, Tolkien noted, "I've always been impressed that we're here surviving because of the indomitable courage of quite small people against impossible odds: jungles, volcanoes, wild beasts. They struggle on, almost blindly in a way. Frodo had very little idea, really. Of course, by the time he'd come to the end of his quest, he was beginning to understand that he was very much more."[2]

FIFTEEN

THE NATURAL (UNNATURAL) WORLD AND LIFE AND DEATH

GENESIS

Whether you view the Judeo-Christian Bible as scripture or a work of literature, the opening words of the Book of Genesis supply a foundation for the creation of the universe. The first lines take us back to a theoretical start of time: no early, no late, nothing but the moment at hand, in perfect step with the newly born concept of *right now*: "In the beginning . . . the Earth was formless and empty."

Over the next few lines, we witness the emergence of light and the separation of light and darkness, establishing night and day, then the first day, providing us with the notion of time moving forward and a way to mark it.

The act of creation, the natural world—including its newly born progression of life and death—and nature personified as a rival or combatant are themes that have inspired writers throughout the centuries (which can gleefully be said because time is now a thing!).

THE LAMB AND THE TYGER

London-born poet William Blake (1757–1827), an accomplished painter and printmaker, was moved by his love of children's literature to create a pair of closely related volumes of poetry, *Songs of Innocence* (1789) and *Songs of Experience* (1794), in which Blake explores the idea of creation. Two of his pieces reflect on animals with opposing natures. In a poem from *Songs of Innocence*, Blake begins,

> Little Lamb who made thee
>   Dost thou know who made thee . . .
> Gave thee clothing of delight,
> Softest clothing wooly bright;
> Gave thee such a tender voice

The line is incredibly striking, asking an animal as kindly and docile as a lamb to describe its origin. The audience has contemplated its own origins since the beginning of time, bringing us closer to the work.

However, Blake doesn't expect an answer in this one-way dialogue, so he supplies his own:

> Little Lamb I'll tell thee!
> He is called by thy name, . . .
> . . . calls himself a Lamb

The poet is alluding to the well-recognized portrayal of the Christian God as a lamb, representing tenderness, peace, and unconditional love.

But in *Songs of Experience*, Blake juxtaposes the image of the lamb beside that of a fearsome tiger:

> Tyger Tyger, burning bright,
> In the forests of the night;
> What immortal hand or eye,
> Could frame thy fearful symmetry?

The image of an orange tiger burning so brightly that it could light up a darkened forest jumps off the page. Coupled with the repetition of "Tyger Tyger" and the alliterative string of *t*'s, *b*'s, and *f*'s, the swiftly flowing and appealing sounds seep into our minds, not to be easily forgotten. Blake then closes his opening pair of lines with "symmetry," which not only describes the tiger but also the stunning balance of what the author has just written.

Blake rightfully inquires on behalf of the reader,

Did he smile his work to see?
Did he who made the Lamb make thee?

The poems make an amazing pairing, with Blake posing the perfect questions and rightfully leaving the audience to ponder the answer.

Many musicians have explored Blake's rhyme schemes and poetic themes. The Irish rock band U2 recorded a pair of consecutive albums titled *Songs of Innocence* (2014) and *Songs of Experience* (2017), covering many of Blake's themes, such as childlike innocence and optimism, eventually morphing into a broader and darker view of the world.

> *If you could hold a two-way conversation with just one animal for five minutes and get real answers to your questions, which species would you choose?*

THE CREATURE

The act of creation isn't always widely applauded and hailed as a miracle, especially when the character responsible for that creation is Dr. Victor Frankenstein. Author Mary Shelley's novel *Frankenstein; Or, The Modern Prometheus* (1818) delves into the question of whether human beings are worthy of assuming the role of creator of living things.

Interestingly, Shelley wrote the novel due to a bet she made with a trio of other authors to see who could come up with the most frightening ghost story. Shelley was just a teenager when she started writing *Frankenstein*. The ultimate success of her novel quickly supercharged the horror genre, increasing its popularity and making Shelley the hands-down winner of that bet.

But let's immediately get something straight, because it's such a common trap in which to fall. Frankenstein is not the being brought to life by the process of piecing together body parts from multiple corpses; that individual is called the Creature or Demon. Dr. Victor Frankenstein is the Frankenstein in the novel's title and the true monster of the story.

What does the Creature look like, and why does he strike immediate fear in almost all who view him? Shelley describes the eight-foot-tall being as hideously ugly, with large white teeth; glowing eyes; black lips and hair; and taut, translucent yellowish skin that "barely disguised the workings of the arteries and muscles underneath." In today's world, the Creature would undoubtedly suffer the indignity of being labeled an automatic swipe-left on any sort of dating app.

So let's examine the Creature's first words to his creator, Dr. Frankenstein, after the Creature has experienced society a bit and taught himself to both speak and read. "I expected this reception," said the Demon. "All men hate the wretched; how, then, must I be hated, who am miserable beyond all living things! Yet you, my creator, detest and spurn me, thy creature, to whom thou art bound by ties only dissoluble by the annihilation of one of us."

The Creature squarely puts the burden of his torment on Dr. Frankenstein, who has shirked his responsibilities as a parent who is supposed to provide unconditional love and help his creation to understand the world. It's a perfect opening conversation as the reader is left to debate the role of family ties and who is the real demon in the story.

The novel has an alternative title: *The Modern Prometheus*. Prometheus is from Greek mythology. He is a god of fire who disobeyed the Olympians by giving fire to man. His punishment? Eternal torment.

Will this be the same punishment ultimately endured by Dr. Frankenstein for *stealing* the act of creation and bringing it to the human realm? The alternative title serves as another opening line, setting the stage to come for readers who know the story of Prometheus. Quite clever on Shelley's part, don't you think?

DIGGING DEEP

Mexican American poet Ada Limón examines the grandeur of creation, not aboveground, but below, in "Notes on the Below" (2016), dedicated to Mammoth Cave National Park in Kentucky. "This poem came out of [an] . . . almost urgent need to point back to the earth," said Limón, a native of Sonoma, California. "We have done so much harm in this life—to one another, to the ground we think we own—and I wanted the chance to speak directly to a sacred place and look for answers, or to simply lay my buzzing mind down at the mercy of the earth's core."[1]

The poem's speaker starts with a question:

> Humongous cavern, tell me, wet limestone, sandstone caprock,
>   bat-wing, sightless translucent cave shrimp,
>
> this endless plummet into more of the unknown,
>   how one keeps secrets for so long.

Why is this opening line so spot-on? The author didn't choose to use such adjectives as *colossal*, *immense*, or *giant* to describe the cavern. Instead, she chose *humongous*, which isn't too far off from *human* and *among us*, making our conversation with the deep Earth more personal. There's also a terrific bleeding of all the cavern's separate elements and inhabitants coming together to create a singular entity. The line is less of a conversation starter and more of a prayerful plea to an entity with superior knowledge, something immense in its stature and internal strength—something far superior to us:

> Tell me what it is...
>   To be the thing not touched by light (no that's not it)
> to not even need the light?... I envy that.

The cavern hasn't answered, but its presence is undeniable:

> tell me,
>
> what it is to be quiet, and yet still breathing.

For answers to questions as meaningful as these, the speaker is not above bowing down and paying deference, with that relationship already established in the opening line:

> I am at the mouth of the cave. I am willing to crawl.

NEVER-ENDING SUMMER

Here's a look at one of William Shakespeare's sonnets with an opening line that has long captured the imagination of readers. In Sonnet 18, the Bard compares the object of his affection to a beautiful, sunlit day in summer—one that never diminishes. It begins,

> Shall I compare thee to a summer's day?
> Thou art more lovely and more temperate.

Shakespeare's metaphor—his direct comparison—comes in the form of a question, asking permission to bring such lofty praise on the subject. Shakespeare chooses to use the word *more* twice for emphasis. He could have used the word *lovelier* instead of *more lovely* and gotten to the correct syllable count (each of the fourteen lines in a sonnet contains ten syllables). But this approach was *more* flattering.

Temperate? It's another way of saying pleasant or mild. So the poet isn't speaking about a ninety-nine-degree scorcher of a day.

If summer gives us a season by which to mark time, can fall and winter be too far behind? Not in Shakespeare's opinion:

> And every fair from fair sometime declines,...
> But thy eternal summer shall not fade.

How long will this be true?

> So long as men can breathe or eyes can see

Now that's a declaration of admiration and love, all building off the perfectly stated metaphor in the opening line.

MURDERING SLEEP

There's the natural order of the universe, and then there's the nature of humankind, often fraught with weaknesses and dark obsessions, usually over acquiring wealth and power. Shakespeare explored such themes in *The Tragedy of Macbeth*. It's one of Shakespeare's most performed plays, but you may discover that actors refuse to refer to the production by its title during a run of any show, even backstage while performing *Macbeth*. You see, the superstition has evolved that the simple utterance of *Macbeth* inside of a theater can curse and ruin the production. So thespians instead call it "the Scottish play" because it takes place in Scotland.

The word *fair* is a key in the opening lines of *Macbeth*. A trio of witches are gathered in an isolated and barren setting amid the sound of thunder and lightning to seemingly cast a spell. The First Witch asks,

> When shall we three meet again?
> In thunder, lightning, or in rain?

Eventually, the Third Witch adds,

> There to meet with Macbeth.

At that moment, Macbeth is a Scottish general in the service of King Duncan.

Then the three witches in unison chant,

> Fair is foul, and foul is fair;
> Hover through the fog and filthy air.

Translation? It's a paradox. What's seemingly good is actually bad. What appears honest is really dishonest. And of course, the opposite—what's horribly evil will be disguised as good. It's a literary technique called chiasmus, in which repeating a phrase in reverse order blends the opposites together, diffusing their opposition to one another.

The witches send word to Macbeth that they've had a vision he will become king. Macbeth shares the news with his wife, Lady Macbeth, and moved by the thought of power, Macbeth stabs King Duncan to death in his sleep. The unnatural has taken over: "Foul is fair."

What's Macbeth's cosmic punishment? He becomes an insomniac and can no longer sleep. It's quite appropriate because when he killed Duncan in his sleep, Macbeth murdered his own ability to sleep, as well. It's all amazingly put into motion through the opening lines and the witches' spell. No wonder Shakespeare is reverently called the Bard.

MIDDLE OF THE NIGHT

Four centuries after Shakespeare, writers are still focusing on the theme of sleep in their work, and why not? Sleep is something with which everyone is familiar, whether you consider sleep to be your friend or a somewhat-frustrating experience. Put poet Dana Gioia down in the camp of "frustrating"; at least that's what we should probably infer from his poem "Insomnia" (1986). The poem opens with a bit of personification, allowing the house to speak in the silence of the night as the narrator struggles to fall asleep:

> Now you hear what the house has to say.
> Pipes clanking, water running in the dark,
> the mortgaged walls shifting in discomfort

It's a one-way conversation that couldn't be held at any other time than the middle of the night, with an insomniac tuned in to nothing else but the separate *complaints* of each element of the house. What are those complaints about? We do not know. But does it really matter?

And there's literally no escape because sleep will not arrive to rescue you:

> But now you must listen to the things you own, . . .
> the moving parts about to come undone

Unlike the daytime, when the place is perhaps inhabited by people to whom you should also pay more attention, there is no background noise to block things out:

How many voices have escaped you until now,
the venting furnace, the floorboards underfoot,
the steady accusations of the clock

And now you are hearing it all, maybe for the first time. Or is it a nightly occurrence adding to the speaker's insomnia?

The terrible clarity this moment brings

All of this unwanted confrontation but for a glass of warm milk or a soothing cup of chamomile tea. Oh, yes, and an opening line that subtly brings a talkative house to life. Well done, Dana Gioia. We hope you live in an apartment!

CLINGING TO LIGHT

An essential element of the natural world is the journey from life to death. Writers have focused on this theme since crude drawings told stories on the walls of caves. Welsh poet Dylan Thomas (1914–1953), mentioned in chapter 6 as the writer who inspired Robert Zimmerman to assume the pen name Bob Dylan, penned the classic "Do Not Go Gentle into That Good Night" (1939), describing that narrow space separating life from death.

Thomas's opening lines compare death to the oncoming of night in a stunning literary metaphor:

Do not go gentle into that good night,
Old age should burn and rave at close of day;
Rage, rage against the dying of the light.

The opening line certainly delivers what it promises. There is nothing *gently* moving forward here. Thomas's choice of *burn* and *rave*, and his consecutive use of *rage* give the opening a powerful and purposeful jolt of life while also conveying the fight for continued survival. This is no gentle reminder of the importance of life: This is a command, a call to action to ensure that a battle is waged and won. What an incredible mastery of language, tempo, and emotion—like a high-performance sports car going from zero to sixty miles per hour the moment your foot hits the gas—in merely twenty-six words!

Like the chorus of a song, Thomas reuses two of his first three opening lines at the end of the poem's five remaining stanzas:

> Do not go gentle into that good night
> Rage, rage against the dying of the light

The poem is tightly packed with spirit and unrestrained energy. "Rage, rage" over gentleness. After all, it's a fight for life and not for the weak of heart.

REVISITING EMILY

Here's another poem by Emily Dickinson, "I Heard a Fly Buzz" (1862), one with quite a unique perspective. The narrator is speaking to us postdeath. In a brilliant and attention-grabbing opening line, Dickinson captures the audience with a statement rarely communicated:

> I heard a Fly buzz—when I died—

The opening line is magnificent because it's presented in such a matter-of-fact way. It should be a once-in-a-lifetime experience (even in death), but Dickinson's delivery is so superbly understated that it completely draws in the audience. It is a riveting paradoxical suggestion. Can you really hear after you've died?

The speaker is observing their own deathbed and the mourners in attendance. And the speaker's final moments?

> There interposed a Fly—

> With Blue—uncertain stumbling Buzz—
> Between the light—and me—
> And then the Windows failed—and then
> I could not to see—

Are the windows the speaker's eyes? Was the light a heavenly paradise? Does the speaker have sight at this moment? From where is the speaker communicating to us?

In lieu of those answers, we are left with the simple buzzing of a fly to ponder, in the huge shadow of an immeasurable opening line. Thank you, Emily.

GRAVEYARD BALLAD

Singer/songwriter Tom T. Hall (1936–2021) grew up in the small town of Olive Hill, Kentucky, where as a young man, he worked in a local graveyard helping to dig graves. Hall is known for his songs that tell a story, and one of his best story songs, "Ballad of Forty Dollars" (1968), takes place just prior to a funeral. The speaker, also a graveyard worker, is sitting in his truck as the mourners arrive:

> The man who preached the funeral
> Said it really was a simple way to die
> He laid down to rest one afternoon
> And never opened up his eyes

Without a stitch of hyperbole, Hall's opening pair of lines tells a simple tale in ordinary language, as if he were standing next to you at the checkout line of the local grocery store. The rhyme of *die* and *eyes* isn't perfect, but it's conversational and free flowing, as though the speaker wasn't even trying to rhyme. That's casual writing at its best.

The speaker and his coworkers had previously dug the grave and carried over chairs for the mourners:

> It took us seven hours
> And I guess we must've drunk a case of beer

The speaker knows the deceased well but stays in his truck and doesn't join the procession to pay his respects:

> I guess I ought to go and watch them put him down
> But I don't own a suit . . .
> Anyway, when they're all through
> I've got to go to work and mow the grass

When the funeral is finally over and the mourners leave, the speaker sums up his private feelings:

> I guess you'd just call it my bad luck
> I hope he rests in peace, the trouble is
> The fellow owes me forty bucks

There are zero pretentions here, no false sentiments—all set up by a simple and perfectly conceived opening line.

Sorry Tom T., I guess you're not getting paid back. Only the listener comes out ahead here—the way it should be.

DEBATING AN ENDING

Because this chapter begins by exploring works that deal with creation, it seems only fitting to end on the theme of total destruction (though it's obviously something I don't endorse—just a literary discussion, mind you). Robert Frost's short poem "Fire and Ice" (1920) debates how the world might end. The opening line is

> Some say the world will end in fire,
> Some say in ice.

It's actually a subtle choice offered to the reader, who is most likely leaning one way or the other internally. That's how to hook an audience—the entire audience, no matter which way they lean.

Frost continues

> From what I've tasted of desire
> I hold with those who favor fire.

Really? The poet's name is Frost! Wasn't he supposed to choose ice?

Before it's over (the poem, not the world), though, Frost doubles back:

> But if it had to perish twice,
> I think I know enough of hate
> To know that for destruction ice
> Is also great
> And would suffice.

The diplomatic poet chose both options. What a politician. So no matter your personal choice, know that Robert Frost agrees with you.

SIXTEEN

SOCIETY AND ITS INFLUENCES

Society can lead us in many different directions, either because of or despite our starting points in life. The possible destinations are countless, with perhaps our social and economic status casting the largest shadow over where we begin the journey. Writers of fiction and nonfiction have been passionate about documenting the rungs on the ladder of class—with their protagonists rising and falling—examining the concept of *how the world might view us* compared to *how we view ourselves.*

THREE THE EASY/HARD WAY

Let's look at a trio of pieces that assign their speakers different starting points in society and how the artists' opening lines give us better insight into those voices.

F. Scott Fitzgerald's novel *The Great Gatsby* (1925), set in early-1920s America, explores the meaning of "great wealth" and whether money can buy happiness. The narrator is Nick Carraway (do you think he'll get *carried away* by what he sees?), who moves in next door to the mysterious millionaire (in that era, the equivalent of a billionaire today) Jay Gatsby, known for his insanely over-the-top parties on his huge estate.

The novel opens with Nick thinking about the advice that his father once gave him: "Whenever you feel like criticizing anyone ... just remember that all the people in this world haven't had the advantages that you've had." We don't know exactly what those "advantages" are yet. Are they monetary, social, physical, emotional, or any one of a myriad of other possibilities? And what about Jay Gatsby? Was he born rich, or did he arrive at his fortune by some other means?

We soon discover that Jay Gatsby doesn't really enjoy himself at his own parties. There is obviously something severely lacking in his life. And after the opening piece of advice from Nick's father, that still-unidentified comparison becomes amplified as we move forward, as Fitzgerald masterfully sets the stage for the reader. Here's a version of *people born with an advantage* on steroids.

New Zealand–born singer/songwriter Lorde, whose real name is Ella Marija Lani Yelich-O'Connor, took her stage name from a personal fascination with the aristocracy. At age thirteen, Lorde penned the song "Royals" (2013), cowritten by Joel Little, showing how the reality of her life was immensely different from *their* world. The opening lines make no apology for a young life lived in the absence of a disposable income:

> I've never seen a diamond in the flesh
> I cut my teeth on wedding rings in the movies.

The juxtaposition of reality and film-inspired fantasy helps the speaker to define this seemingly cold and distant relationship between everyday people and those of society's highest tier. Consider the unique images and phrasing. The absence of ever seeing a diamond "in the flesh" and "cutting my teeth" makes the nonexperience/experience both personal and physical for the speaker:

> Cristal, Maybach, diamonds on your timepiece
> ... tigers on a gold leash

The excess can be unimaginable and barely relatable. How about the lavish and televised weddings of king and queens, princes and princesses?

> We don't care, we aren't caught up in your love affair.

And why should the speaker care? Other than a fairy-tale glass-slipper romance, it's a closed door to becoming a royal. Just ask Meghan

Markle, a commoner who married Britain's Prince Harry, before the couple moved to the United States and relinquished their royal titles:

> And we'll never be royals
> It don't run in our blood
> That kind of luxe just ain't for us

Society's biggest shame is undoubtedly the condoning of slavery for far too long. Frederick Douglass (who died in 1895 at the approximate age of seventy-eight) was born a slave in Maryland. But Douglass eventually became a statesmen, social reformer, and writer who wrote three autobiographies about his life. The author begins his work *Narrative of the Life of Frederick Douglass, an American Slave* (1845) with a subtle societal difference between the lives of slaves as compared to people born free: "I have no accurate knowledge of my age, never having seen any authentic record containing it. By far the larger part of the slaves know as little of their ages as horses know of theirs, and it is the wish of most masters within my knowledge to keep their slaves thus ignorant."

At the onset, Douglass immediately conveys to his audience the concept of a fourth-class citizenship, equating his treatment to that of livestock beneath an owner. His honesty pushes the narrative forward at an accelerated pace, with no wasted words or superfluous feelings:

> I do not remember to have ever met a slave who could tell of his birthday. They seldom come nearer to it than planting-time, harvest-time, cherry-time, spring-time, or fall-time. A want of information concerning my own was a source of unhappiness to me even during childhood. The white children could tell their ages. I could not tell why I ought to be deprived of the same privilege.

Deprived is a powerful word choice, evoking a depth of emotion at what was denied to Douglass due to the color of his skin. With this forceful introduction, Douglass's opening, which is devoid of physical violence, gives the reader insight into how small societal differences can have huge psychological effects.

> *Was there ever something you really wanted in life? Not something you could purchase in a store or online but rather something more intrinsic? Did you ever obtain it? How did either possessing it or not possessing it influence your life?*

PRIVILEGE: PLUS OR HANDICAP?

Here is a pair of pieces—one of the world's most recognized rock songs and an iconic poem—that delve into the societal concept of privilege and debate whether having it in your life is a perk or impediment. Guitarist Jimmy Page of the British rock band Led Zeppelin composed a stunning melody for which his bandmate, lyricist and singer Robert Plant, felt compelled to find the right words. The completed song is "Stairway to Heaven" (1971). The opening line describes a woman of privilege who believes she knows what life and possibly the afterlife is all about. And for her, it's not that deep or complicated. It's seemingly owed her:

> There's a lady who's sure all that glitters is gold
> And she's buying a stairway to Heaven

The image of a stairway to paradise and redemption seems incredible, something everybody might desire. But the lyrics certainly paint this lady, a British woman of social rank and privilege, as someone not to be envied but for whom the audience should feel pity. After all, she's gullible, believing "all that glitters is gold," and misguided, thinking she can buy her way into heaven.

How affluent and advantaged is she? Even in heaven she believes that she'll be better than most:

> When she gets there she knows, if the stores are all closed
> With a word she can get what she came for

We're later warned to look at ourselves as we travel down life's road, to make sure that, like this woman, we don't find ourselves believing "our shadows taller than our soul." There's a lot to think about here for a rock-and-roll anthem, spurred on by an opening line that totally encapsulates the protagonist for us.

Here's a glimpse at a different image of a staircase detailed by Langston Hughes in his poem "Mother to Son" (1922). The opening line is advice by a mother, who has obviously lived a life very much unlike the "lady" in the previous piece:

> Well, son, I'll tell you:
> Life for me ain't been no crystal stair.

The mother's use of the word *ain't* gives us a clue that, outwardly, she'd be considered by society to be in a lower strata. Not only wasn't the staircase made of crystal, but it also seems fashioned by society to make her stop climbing, to halt her progress:

> It had tacks in it,
> And splinters,
> And boards torn up

The mother warns her son not to become discouraged, that there's no time to rest because there's an urgency to get to someplace better—a place neither has yet seen. And the mother leads by example:

> So boy, don't you turn back.
> Don't you set down on the steps . . .
> I's still climbin'

The image in the opening line is so important that Hughes, through the words of the mother, feels compelled to restate it for emphasis at the poem's closure:

> And life for me ain't been no crystal stair.

THE BURDEN OF FAME

A relatively small number of people in the world gain true fame—not in their *own* minds, but in many of *ours* and in the media. It's an aspect of society that often makes little sense. Why would fans idolize those with whom they most likely have nothing in common? And what about the concept of fame itself? Is it a magic carpet ride or a speeding roller coaster that at any moment could hurtle off the tracks and out of control?

Artists have used the theme of fame in their work extensively, perhaps because many of them have experienced both the positive and negative aspects of it. I present a pair of hit songs that deal with fame, in Elton John and Bernie Taupin's "Candle in the Wind" (1973) and Eminem's "Stan" (2009).

"Candle in the Wind" tracks the life of media icon Marilyn Monroe, whose real name was Norma Jeane Mortenson. The opening line meticulously uses her birth name in order to pay tribute to the *real* person behind the Hollywood glitz:

> Goodbye, Norma Jeane,
> Though I never knew you at all

It's a heartfelt farewell to a star who had passed away more than a decade prior to the song's debut, when John was seventeen, and Taupin, just fourteen.

The song's narrative voice isn't naive to the fact that we don't really *know* media stars and their happiness and hardships. We normally just see a packaged image of them. But the speaker feels as if he can see past that veil, and that's a vital bonding mechanism with those in the audience who have a similar perspective:

> You had the grace to hold yourself
> While those around you crawled
> ... out of the woodwork

John and Taupin juxtapose Norma Jeane's natural grace with the industry types who crawled out of the woodwork, seemingly like cockroaches, to affix themselves to her rising popularity.

Even when she died of a drug overdose, the press that helped to make her a star milked every last media moment they could out of her sad demise:

> All the papers had to say
> Was that Marilyn was found in the nude

Transporting himself back in time, watching her perform from a seat a great distance from the stage, John sings,

> Goodbye, Norma Jeane
> From the man in the 22nd row
> Who sees you as something more than sexual
> More than just our Marilyn Monroe

In 1997, John and Taupin rewrote the song for Princess Diana, who perished in an automobile accident while being pursued by paparazzi—a victim of her own unwanted fame and media appeal. It was titled "Candle in the Wind 1997." The opening line was changed to

> Goodbye England's rose
> May you ever grow in our hearts

In the rap "Stan," Marshall Mathers III, who goes by the name Eminem, explores one of the most testing aspects of fame in a multi-speaker piece about a fan who wants to communicate more than just well wishes. Inspired by real-life fan communications received by the rapper, the opening lines begin with a tone that's too familiar and somewhat disturbing. A fan named Stan writes to his rap hero. This is his opening line:

> Dear Slim, I wrote you but you still ain't callin
> I left my cell, my pager, and my home phone at the bottom

It's a masterful opening that just touches on a tinge of anger, resentment, and instability:

> I know you probably hear this every day, but I'm your biggest fan

Eminem perfectly captures how some fans try to put themselves closer to the artists, relate their lives, and even attempt to gain access to them. It's real, and it's both flattering and frightening.

Months down the line, with Stan not hearing a response from Slim, the correspondence starts to take a more aggressive tone, as seen in the salutation:

> Dear Mister-I'm-Too-Good-To-Call-Or-Write-My-Fans

The upcoming twist here is that Slim eventually answers in a conciliatory tone:

> Dear Stan, I meant to write you sooner but I just been busy

He sends along an autographed cap and goes on to tell his superobsessed fan that he probably needs to get his act together and worry more about his family than a rapper he's never met.

There's an ending of consequence to "Stan" that I don't want to reveal for anyone who hasn't heard this extremely worthy work yet, with a closing line that should make every uberpopular artist cringe.

> *If you could spend an afternoon with someone famous, who would it be? Do you believe that afternoon would live up to your expectations? Or in the end, might you be disappointed?*

THAT BOOK IS FIRE!

Societies around the world, through many different eras, including today, have fallen into the misguided trap of worrying about which books their adults and adolescents read, creating lists of banned books that don't support their own societal views. In a stark warning against those actions, author Ray Bradbury (1920–2012), a native of Waukegan, Illinois, and a driving force in bringing science fiction into the mainstream, penned *Fahrenheit 451* (1953), a novel in which all books are banned and literally burned on sight, ironically by the fire department.

Why does Bradbury's novel have that title? It is the temperature at which books will burn. And adding at bit of symbolism, it is the number that his protagonist fireman, Guy Montag, wears on his helmet.

Bradbury begins with these lines:

> It was a special pleasure to see things eaten, to see things blackened and changed. With the brass nozzle in his fists, with this great python spitting its venomous kerosene upon the world, the blood pounded in his head, and his hands were the hands of some amazing conductor playing all the symphonies of blazing and burning to bring down the tatters and charcoal ruins of history.

The lines are propelled by a pair of striking images, comparing the firehose to a venomous snake and Guy Montag to a musical conductor about to lead a symphony orchestra in a tragic score of destruction. That's how to grab an audience's attention and emotions.

Bradbury has even conceived of an eight-legged robotic dog that helps the fire department to sniff out hidden books: "Next, [Montag] flicked the igniter and the house jumped up in a gorging fire that burned the evening sky red and yellow and black. . . . He wanted above all, like the old joke, to shove a marshmallow on a stick in the furnace, while the flapping pigeon-winged books died on the porch and lawn of the house."

As in every good story, there's internal drama, and Guy Montag starts to have serious thoughts as to whether he's really doing the right thing and is on the correct side of this antiknowledge-fueled society.

> *Do you believe that other people (society) should have a role in deciding what you can or can't read? Or is that a decision best left to the individual?*

SEVENTEEN

WAR

War is the ultimate struggle between life and death, freedom and bondage, and often good versus evil. Armed conflicts have been both a blight on our society and a last resort to preserve human dignity, showcasing the best and worst qualities humankind has to offer. Artists have presented the theme of war in their work from many angles, including their firsthand experiences standing directly in the line of fire, either as combatants or as war correspondents. I present several such war-themed works and show how these artists' opening lines and sequences are meant to focus the audience for the often harshly explicit journey to come.

HEAVY JACKET

The film *Full Metal Jacket* (1987) follows a platoon of US Marine recruits through their boot camp training on Parris Island, South Carolina. The movie is based on a novel *The Short-Timers* (1979) by Marine Corps veteran Gustav Hasford, who is joined on the screenplay by Michael Herr and Stanley Kubrick. The term *full metal jacket* describes a bullet or projectile encased in an outer shell made of a harder metal, allowing it to be fired at a higher velocity.

In the film, the audience first catches a glimpse of the recruits getting buzz cuts at the base barbershop—leaving all with the exact same haircut, deemphasizing any thought of individuality, an example of esprit de corps, a strong honor and regard for the group, not one's self.

The first full-fledged scene opens with the platoon in their barracks, standing at attention in front of their bunks as the drill instructor less than cordially introduces himself: "I am Gunnery Sergeant Hartman, your senior drill instructor. From now on, you will speak only when spoken to, and the first and last words out of your filthy sewers will be 'Sir!' Do you maggots understand that?"

The imagery here is amazing, with an instructor named "Heart-man" putting the hammer down. The recruits are mere "maggots," and their mouths, "filthy sewers." And they haven't even made a mistake in their training yet. It's a trio of opening lines that lets the audience know this is for real—no coddling, no babysitting, just intensity.

Sergeant Hartman continues with his pleasantries: "If you survive recruit training . . . you will be a weapon, you will be a minister of death, praying for war. But until that day, you are pukes! You're the lowest form of life on Earth." The platoon is going to be dehumanized, turned into instruments of death. We're not anywhere near a battlefield—still in the safety of the barracks—and it's nothing but zealousness. And obviously, coscreenwriter Hasford lived this type of scene. That's authenticity in writing!

WAR AND LAUGHS

The comedy-drama *M*A*S*H* (1972–1983) ran on TV for eleven seasons, making a monumental impact on society through both its portrayal of the horrors of war (set during the Korean War) and the comic madness in which the military/medical personnel indulged in order to maintain their sanity. The title is an acronym for *Mobile Army Surgical Hospital*. Though the show stopped production in 1983, it continues on in syndication, having never been off the airwaves since its debut.

The TV show was inspired by the 1970 feature film of the same name, which in turn was based on the book *MASH: A Novel about Three Army Doctors* by H. Richard Hornberger, a former wartime army surgeon using the nom de plume Richard Hooker.

Combining comedy with poignant drama is an extremely difficult task. Here's how famed screenwriter Larry Gelbart achieved it through the opening two minutes of the show's initial episode:

A note on the screen introduces the setting as "Korea, 1950."

A pair of military officers are playing golf, wearing the odd combination of army shoes and brightly colored Hawaiian shirts. (Golf in a war zone? Yes, they're hitting golf balls into a field of land mines.)

A male surgeon and a female nurse appear to be laboring over a patient in an operating room, but as the camera pulls back, they're actually opening a bottle of champagne. As the cork on that bottle pops, one of those golf balls explodes a land mine, perfectly juxtaposing the best and the worst of loud noises in wartime.

A few seconds later, a game of touch football in the compound is interrupted by the sound of helicopters bringing in casualties from the nearby battlefront.

Over the camp loudspeaker, a voice announces, "Attention all personnel, report immediately to admitting ward and operating room!"

It's a delicate and brilliant balance achieved by Gelbart, like a tightrope walker negotiating the high wire without a safety net in heavy winds. You just have to applaud his skills in bringing everything together in a succinct opening scene in the show's debut.

What kind of impact did *M*A*S*H* make over its more than a decade on the air? Some 77 percent of the TVs in the United States were tuned into the final episode, making it a shared cultural event.

> How might you have used humor as a relief in some of life's tensest moments?

ANTIWAR ANTHEM

"War" (1970) is a classic soul/protest song written by Norman Whitfield and Barrett Strong and performed by a myriad of musical groups and individual artists. Why is it so popular? Unfortunately, wars seem to never go out of style, and there's a continual need for musicians to make a statement against them.

In their lyrics, Whitfield and Barrett are direct and to the point:

War, huh, yeah
What is it good for
Absolutely nothing

No images. No allusions. No flowery language nor poetry. In fact, the *huh*, a vocalization of disgust and displeasure, expresses an emotion that words could not. The opening line is an assessment of war with which few people could pose an argument.

DIFFERENT PATHS, SAME DESTINATION

Let's consider a pair of poems that speak to us in very different language and images yet ultimately present the same question: When will there be peace?

Here's how Denise Levertov from Essex, England, begins her poem "Making Peace" (1987):

> A voice from the dark called out,
>   "The poets must give us
> imagination of peace, to oust the intense, familiar
> imagination of disaster."

It's a plea of near hopelessness. Imagine calling for poets to solve the problem of war and not political leaders or armed soldiers to keep the peace? I'm sure most readers are asking themselves, "Poets?" And it may take them a split second to realize, everyone else has repeatedly failed at the task, so why not the poets?

The voice from the dark isn't searching for a momentary ceasefire. It's asking for something that can shape the minds of people and make a truly lasting impression. The voice desires

> "Peace, not only
> the absence of war."

The ambitious request is internalized by the writer, and Levertov answers as both a poet and a realist who understands the hard work involved:

> But peace, like a poem,
> is not there ahead of itself,
> can't be imagined before it is made

It's a conclusion that owes its weight and impact to the perfectly phrased plea of the opening line.

Poet Brian Turner served in the US military for seven years, in such war-torn settings as Bosnia-Herzegovina and Iraq. His poem

"The Hurt Locker" (2005), meaning a place of deep pain, immediately focuses on what lies in the wake of war:

> Nothing but hurt left here.
> Nothing but bullets and pain

It's a start that leaves you nothing in the way comfort or even a shred of hope. And then, just when the reader is most likely imagining the families and children suffering amid the devastation, the author deftly drives us further back on our unprepared heels:

> Believe it when a twelve-year-old
> rolls a grenade into the room.

The horror and loss of innocence is mindboggling. Is there even anything left to lose? Yes, is the author's answer to that question:

> Open the hurt locker and learn
> how rough men come hunting for souls.

Turner certainly doesn't deceive the reader with the bleakness of his opening lines. Instead, he ultimately prepares them to receive an ending as harsh as this one.

DESERVING BETTER

Illinois native John Prine (1946–2020), a critically acclaimed singer/songwriter for nearly a half century, was once a US postal employee who wrote his earliest songs while delivering mail along his route. Prine penned the song "Sam Stone" (1971) about a US veteran who came home from war with a serious drug addiction, one that would affect not only his life but also his family's. It starts,

> Sam Stone came home to his wife and family
> After serving in the conflict overseas

It's a simple beginning with the alliteration of the protagonist's name ringing in the audience's ears—*Sam Stone* (plus *serving, overseas*). Then there's the surname *Stone*, as in *he's either made of stone or is too often stoned* hanging there for the taking:

> And the time that he served had shattered all his nerves

Sam Stone has obviously endured some intense situations in the service of his country. So what kind of help and counseling do we have for this hero?

> The morphine eased the pain . . .
> And gave him all the confidence he lacked
> With a Purple Heart and a monkey on his back

It's a statement on many levels—from the horrors of war to drug addiction, to posttraumatic stress disorder (PTSD), to the woefully insufficient services for our wounded vets returning home. And it's all built on the straightforward, no-nonsense tone of the opening line grabbing our attention: "Sam Stone came home."

Sadly, John Prine was one of the first artists to pass away from COVID-19, on April 7, 2020.

WAR HAWK

Not every work is blatantly antiwar. There will always be voices and characters gravitating toward the so-called glory of battle, almost relishing it. Case in point: the 1970 biographical war film *Patton*, which examines the life of General George S. Patton, who commanded several US Army divisions during World War II.

In the film, Patton is played by legendary actor George C. Scott, with the screenplay written by Francis Ford Coppola and Edmund North. The opening sequence is one of the most recognized in the history of film. It's admired for its combination of visual and verbal imagery and how it opens the door into the psyche of the protagonist.

It begins with General Patton, who is decked out in full military regalia and even described in the script as looking like a "peacock," standing in front of a huge American flag that fills the entire screen. Along with his troops, Patton salutes the flag as the national anthem plays.

At the anthem's conclusion, he addresses *his* troops: "Now, I want you to remember that no bastard ever won a war by dying for his country. He won it by making the other poor dumb bastard die for his country." It's a mirthful math equation from the mind of someone who sees soldiers as pawns on a chess board, momentarily forgetting about their humanity.

Patton continues, "Men, all this stuff you've heard about America not wanting to fight, wanting to stay out of the war, is a lot of horse dung. Americans traditionally love to fight. All real Americans love the sting of battle." The protagonist is trying to sell his troops on the notion that a *real* American will embrace the pain that comes with war. Through the opening five lines of dialogue, the screenwriters have already established a one-way relationship between a demigod like General Patton and the troops he will eventually order into battle, knowing many will not return alive.

EIGHTEEN

DYSTOPIAN LANDSCAPES

I made a point to have the discussion on dystopian landscapes follow the chapter on war. After all, if society as we know it ever ceased to exist—followed by some abhorrent mutation of a society either without laws or with new ones that abolish our freedoms—the most likely cause would be a world war punctuated by the use of multiple nuclear weapons.

Artists have written extensively about these darkened future societies, or society-less frontiers. Sometimes their surrounding landscapes appear amazingly similar to our own, while others are portrayed as barren wastelands, with water, food, and shelter in short supply. Whether it is apes ruling over humankind or machines making us obsolete and therefore no longer needed, the vision of artists in all genres leaves us with a discerning and sometimes worrisome eye on the future.

WOMEN AND UNWOMEN

Canadian author Margaret Atwood set her dystopian novel *The Handmaid's Tale* (1985) in the not too distant future. The US government no longer exists, overthrown by a political group that believes men should rule and women should serve. Men called the commanders are at the top of the new food chain in a highly patriarchal society. They hold the power and have totally stripped women and unwomen, now the lowest class of citizen, of all essential rights. Females cannot have money, own property, read, or write. And women who are still fertile may fall into the guarded position of becoming handmaids for the new elite while sacrificing further freedoms.

CHAPTER EIGHTEEN

Atwood's opening lines harken back to a time not long ago when the gymnasium housing the handmaids might have hosted a high school basketball game or a dance. The protagonist, Offred, a captive handmaid, begins,

> I could smell, faintly like an afterimage, the pungent scent of sweat, shot through with the sweet taint of chewing gum and perfume from the watching girls, felt-skirted as I knew from pictures, later in miniskirts, then pants, then in one earring, spiky green-streaked hair. Dances would have been held there; the music lingered . . . style upon style, an undercurrent of drums . . . garlands made of tissue-paper flowers, cardboard devils, a revolving ball of mirrors, powdering the dancers with a snow of light.

The freedom to dance, to dream of romance and to dress the way you wanted—all gone now. But Offred's recollections of the past subtly gives the audience hope that this horrific new society can be challenged.

The name *Offred*? It literally means *of Fred*, property of a commander named Fred.

How did Atwood come to envision this society in *The Handmaid's Tale*? Is it totally invented, or does it have elements of an historical basis? "I made a rule for myself: I would not include anything that human beings had not already done in some other place or time, or for which the technology did not already exist," noted Atwood.

> I did not wish to be accused of dark, twisted inventions, or of misrepresenting the human potential for deplorable behavior. The group-activated hangings, the tearing apart of human beings, the clothing specific to castes and classes, the forced childbearing and the appropriation of the results, the children stolen by regimes and placed for upbringing with high-ranking officials, the forbidding of literacy, the denial of property rights—all had precedents, and many of these were to be found, not in other cultures and religions, but within Western society.[1]

FEED THE HUNGRY, BUT JUST SOME OF THEM

Katniss Everdeen is the teen protagonist and narrator of *The Hunger Games* (2008), a novel by Suzanne Collins, a native of Hartford, Connecticut. Collins immediately zeros the reader in on a loving family in a challenging environment where the comforts we take for granted will most likely be absent. Katniss begins, "When I wake up, the other side of the bed is cold. My fingers stretch out, seeking Prim's warmth but finding only the rough canvas cover of the mattress." No blankets? No bedding? Just a rough canvas cover on which to sleep. And the warmth of her little sister Primrose is somehow missing.

Katniss muses, "She must have had bad dreams and climbed in with our mother. Of course, she did. This is the day of the reaping." So nightmares are not an uncommon occurrence. And their mother is portrayed as a source of added protection for Prim, making the child feel secure enough to close her eyes again.

The day of the reaping? Soon the reader learns that later today, human tributes will be chosen via lottery to compete in a battle to the death called the Hunger Games. Two participants, ages twelve to eighteen, are chosen from each of the twelve districts. The lone survivor of the nationally televised event wins food and supplies for their district to satisfy the hungry and poor, which is pretty much everyone except for those who run the government from the Capitol. Naturally, they're the sponsors of this depraved contest.

And this year, Prim, now twelve years old, is eligible to be selected.

It's a simple yet incredibly revealing opening paragraph—four sentences that start to shape the audience's perceptions of the type of society we are about to experience alongside the Everdeen family. Directly on the heels of that paragraph, we hear about Katniss's hunting boots and her ability to put food on the table with a bow and arrow, a skill learned from her departed father. And this foreshadowing should already leave the reader pondering how the ability to hunt will propel Katniss forward in this rapidly unfolding story. "Happy Hunger Games! And may the odds be ever in your favor!"

Collins also penned a pair of sequels to *The Hunger Games*—*Catching Fire* (2009) and *Mockingjay* (2010). The trilogy was also made into films.

> Do you think you could survive in the wilderness, needing to find your own food and water and create your own shelter? On which of your skills would you most rely to accomplish that?

A SECOND CHANCE

If you knew that the end of humankind wasn't too many sunrises away, within the span of a young man's lifetime, what would you personally risk to prevent it from happening? That's the premise of the film *Terminator 2: Judgment Day* (1991) written by James Cameron and William Wisher. It's the sequel to *The Terminator* (1984), in which Arnold Schwarzenegger portrays an unstoppable machine sent back in time to murder Sarah Connor before she can give birth to John Connor, the leader of the future resistance that will one day overcome the machines.

The supremely interesting aspect of Cameron and Wisher's opening visuals and dialogue is that the pair show you the absolute reality of a gutted and charred Earth, where glowing-eyed machines rule with one goal programmed into them: exterminate what's left of the human race. The opening shot is a daylight scene of crowded downtown Los Angeles. Hordes of cars, bumper to bumper. People intent on going about their busy day. But that view slowly dissolves into a nighttime scene of the same place. Only now it's a darkened postapocalyptic landscape. Skyscrapers shattered. Sidewalks turned to rubble. Everywhere we see the pooled remains of metal that had gone molten and the skinless skeletons of people who probably never saw the attack coming.

Then we get the explanation from Sarah Connor, as her voice plays over the destruction: "Three billion human lives ended on August 29th, 1997. The survivors of the nuclear fire called the war 'Judgment Day.' They lived to face a new nightmare—the war against the machines." Sarah informs us that the machines have sent someone back in time to kill her young son, John Connor, since their first plan, to murder her, had failed, but the resistance has also sent someone to protect him: "It was just a question of which one of them would reach him first."

For a moment, we're rescued from that future ashen world. We're back before it happened, where both Terminators Sarah described are about to arrive. So now we have a chance at saving the planet by saving this boy. What a way to disarm a potential apocalypse and what a rooting interest for the audience. And it was all brought together in perfect balance by the screenwriters' opening scenes and dialogue.

The twist here? Schwarzenegger plays the "good" Terminator sent to protect young John Connor. A classic case of role reversal!

OPPOSITE LAND

How would you like to be prosecuted for simply thinking about a crime, especially one against the government? Prosecuted by whom, you ask? Why the Thought Police. Who else?

That's the basis of a dystopian world created by British author George Orwell in his novel *Nineteen Eighty-Four* (1949). Does the book take place in 1984? That's hard to say because we can't trust the official government calendar to be correct, as the republic of Oceania and its dictator, named Big Brother, manipulate many facts about their society through the Ministry of Truth. That's right, the Ministry of *Truth* tells lies.

Orwell's protagonist is Winston Smith, a midlevel worker for the Ministry of Truth who in his heart secretly hates the government and every bit of repression for which it stands. Here's how the author describes Winston's arrival to his seventh-floor walkup apartment in the opening lines: "It was a bright cold day in April, and the clocks were striking thirteen. Winston Smith, his chin nuzzled into his breast in an effort to escape the vile wind, slipped quickly through the glass doors of Victory Mansions, though not quickly enough to prevent a swirl of gritty dust from entering along with him."

The clocks were striking thirteen? So it's a society with some immediate differences from ours. Unfortunately, the correct time is the least of Winston's worries. The fact that he can't escape the "vile wind" or even the "gritty dust," which enters the apartment building with him, signals to the audience that Winston is constantly in the presence of someone or something virtually unshakable.

It's not long until we're introduced to the massive posters of Big Brother, with the caption "BIG BROTHER IS WATCHING YOU." There is also a telescreen in Winston's apartment that both plays propaganda messages and can watch his every move: "Winston kept his back turned to the telescreen. It was safer; though, as he well knew, even a back can be revealing." Besides Winston's inner feelings against the government, he's also keeping a diary, which is absolutely forbidden.

The three party slogans etched in the Ministry of Truth's immense pyramid-like building? "WAR IS PEACE. FREEDOM IS SLAVERY. IGNORANCE IS STRENGTH." All party slogans are always in capitals for emphasis.

In just a half-dozen or so paragraphs, Orwell establishes a paradoxical world of frightening proportions where the individual is always suspect. All that, and our protagonist hasn't even spoken a word yet. Although he shouldn't speak, even while alone at home, because the party is always listening. Does this hit close to home? Sound a little bit like Alexa and Google today?

YOUR TRUE CALLING

You've heard of aptitude tests? You know, where they give you a few pages of simple questions, a few math equations, and then try to tell you the future job for which you might be most qualified: teacher, lawyer, barber, butcher. I suppose it would be quite interesting if you scored out to be a funeral director. Well, that's another discussion.

The future postapocalyptic setting of Chicago in Veronica Roth's novel *Divergent* (2011) makes an old-fashioned aptitude test seem like child's play. The ubercontrolling society in charge has been divided into five factions, and at the age of sixteen, you must join one of them. It's a system that limits independent choice and thinking, keeping teens, one of the most likely sources of revolt in a society, in check.

Each faction highlights a different quality, such as selflessness, peacefulness, honesty, intelligence, and bravery. The family of Roth's protagonist, Beatrice Prior, belongs to the selfless group. Here's how the author describes that household in the opening lines: "There is one mirror in my house. It is behind a sliding panel in the hallway upstairs. Our faction allows me to stand in front of it on the second day of every third month, the day my mother cuts my hair."

Selfless people shouldn't be into vanity, so looking at yourself in a mirror would be a no-no. But Beatrice needs to sneak a peek or two at herself anyway, tipping the reader off that she is a rule breaker who probably won't remain with the selfless faction and will thus be separated from her family.

Beatrice's test results are inconclusive. That makes her a Divergent, fitting into a wide array of possibilities, something feared and persecuted in this society. Imagine being sixteen years old and *not* having your life fully planned out yet? (In case you missed it, that's sarcasm.) I felt the need to remind you in case your better thinking has been unbalanced by all these dystopian worlds.

Being "factionless" means living on the streets as an outcast, so Beatrice begins the agonizing process of figuring out which faction to join and has just twenty-four hours in which to do it. It's a pressure-filled society for teens who are being trained to immerse themselves in groups. Roth's opening line beautifully reflects that, turning the simple activity of a haircut in front of a mirror into a stifling, guilt-ridden process.

> *What are your best qualities as a person and academic subjects as a student? How might that all help you in one day choosing a career? Oh, and no pressure here! Take your time!*

HOORAY, SUCCESS!

You've made it! I hope that you thoroughly enjoyed our shared journey, coming to understand how perfectly penned opening lines in all types of literary endeavors can almost instantly align the audience with the artist's ideas.

Along the way, I hope that you've made a bevy of new friends: Emily Dickinson, Langston Hughes, William Blake, and Maya Angelou, to name just a few. Of course, artistic creations like Miss Luella Bates Washington Jones, Jay Gatsby, Bella Swan, Bilbo Baggins, Huck Finn, Katniss Everdeen, and both Alice and the White Rabbit (who always seems to be running late) need more friends, as well. You can visit them all anytime you want, either online or at your school or local library. (No going down a rabbit or hobbit hole required!)

I hope that this book has also given you some ideas for fun and entertaining projects to pursue. Perhaps you'll parody your favorite film or TV series through a script you plan to write yourself. Just like the kids from the Captain Underpants series, you could start a fledgling comic book company. Maybe you'll choose a Taylor Swift, Olivia Rodrigo, or Beyoncé melody you like and write your own lyrics to it. Or possibly be like Mary Shelley and, even as a teen, write a horror tale that becomes a classic.

But just remember, the next time someone says to you, "Sit down for a moment, I'm going to tell you a story," listen closely. Whether that's a literal phrasing or simply implied because you just filled a seat in a theater, turned on the TV, flipped on some music, or opened a book to read, pay attention to the opening lines. They'll more than likely impart some important information that will enhance the rest of the story to come.

And the next time you write a story of your own, polish those opening lines until they shine with the same sparkle as the rest of your vision.

Once upon a time...

NOTES

CHAPTER TWO

1. Tom Vitale, "Ralph Ellison: No Longer the 'Invisible Man' 100 Years After His Birth," NPR, May 30, 2014, https://www.npr.org/sections/codeswitch/2014/05/30/317056807/ralph-ellison-no-longer-the-invisible-man-100-years-after-his-birth.

CHAPTER THREE

1. Ruth Franklin, "'The Lottery Letters,'" *New Yorker*, June 25, 2013, https://www.newyorker.com/books/page-turner/the-lottery-letters.
2. Stephen King, *On Writing: A Memoir of the Craft* (Scribner, 2000).

CHAPTER FOUR

1. Michael Paulson, "'Hamilton' Heads to Broadway in a Hip-Hop Retelling," *New York Times*, July 12, 2015, https://www.nytimes.com/2015/07/13/theater/hamilton-heads-to-broadway-in-a-hip-hop-retelling.html.

CHAPTER FIVE

1. Brainy Quote, "Neil Armstrong Quotes," accessed February 18, 2025, https://www.brainyquote.com/quotes/neil_armstrong_101138.

CHAPTER NINE

1. Dale Kawashima, "Acclaimed Singer/Songwriter Janis Ian Talks About Her Great Career, from Her Hit 'At Seventeen' to Her New Album, *The Light at the End of the Line*," SongwriterUniverse, January 12, 2023, https://www.songwriteruniverse.com/janis-ian-songs-at-seventeen-light-at-tne-end-of-the-line-2023.htm.

CHAPTER ELEVEN

1. Billy Joel, "New Billy Joel Q&A—Can You Tell Me What Made You Write the Song 'Summer, Highland Falls'?" August 17, 2011, https://www.billyjoel.com/news/new-billy-joel-qa-can-you-tell-me-what-made-you-write-song-summer-highland-falls/.

CHAPTER THIRTEEN

1. Jacob Uitti, "The 13 Best Bill Withers Quotes," American Songwriter, March 15, 2023, https://americansongwriter.com/the-13-best-bill-withers-quotes/.

CHAPTER FOURTEEN

1. Andrew Stump, "Tolkien's 1965 Interview," Quora, 2019, https://tolkienbystump.quora.com/Tolkien-s-1965-Interview.
2. Stump, "Tolkien's 1965 Interview."

CHAPTER FIFTEEN

1. Ada Limón, "Notes on the Below," Poets.org, 2016, https://poets.org/poem/notes-below.

CHAPTER EIGHTEEN

1. Margaret Atwood, "Margaret Atwood on How She Came to Write *The Handmaid's Tale*," Literary Hub, April 25, 2018, https://lithub.com/margaret-atwood-on-how-she-came-to-write-the-handmaids-tale/.

FURTHER READING, LISTENING, VIEWING, AND EXPLORATION

If you're intrigued by the perfectly penned opening lines to the novels, poems, plays, songs, and films you've encountered in this book, then I've got something special for you. The following list will guide you to websites, books, and videos that should provide you with even more to think about and enjoy.

Psst. You can also impress your teachers with these deeper dives and ultimately know more than your classmates. That's just a little something extra from me to you!

CHAPTER ONE

Check out Snoopy's novel. That's right, a dog (really Charles M. Schulz), wrote a novel, *Snoopy and "It Was a Dark and Stormy Night."* It's perhaps the shortest novel in history and is a lot of fun, with an insane ending. Also, check out the comic strips with Snoopy, Charlie Brown, and the rest of the *Peanuts* characters. Because each strip is just a few panels long, every word and drawing has a lot to say. It's artistic economy at its very best!

Like Poe's poem "The Raven"? Then check out *The Simpsons'* "Treehouse of Horror" episode in which Bart Simpson portrays the raven. Find it online. You won't be disappointed.

If songwriter Don McLean has made you curious about Vincent Van Gogh's painting *The Starry Night*, find a photo of it online or in a book featuring Van Gogh's art. See the images that McLean borrowed from the work and featured in his song.

CHAPTER TWO

Intrigued by the lives of such pop stars as Taylor Swift, Billie Eilish, and Olivia Rodrigo? There are a ton of books and articles about them. Look them up at your local library or online. As you most likely know, their songs and music videos are widely available on such platforms as YouTube.

At the 1993 inauguration of incoming President Bill Clinton, Maya Angelou read her poem "On the Pulse of Morning." Check out this brilliant piece of work.

Explore why Melville, Long Island, came to be named after the author of *Moby-Dick*.

Watch the film *Forrest Gump*, and count how many famously historical events you can find in which the lead character is present.

Study up on the horror movie genre, and figure out the difference between Ralph Ellison's *Invisible Man* protagonist and the widely popular Invisible Man (originally created by H. G. Wells), who occasionally throws down with the Wolfman and Dracula in different incarnations.

The poems of Emily Dickinson are normally just a few lines in length. Try reading one a day and perhaps even memorizing it. You can easily find her work in any library or on several websites dedicated to the poet.

CHAPTER THREE

Try an online search of parodies based on Hamlet's "To be or not to be" soliloquy, and see the influence Shakespeare's rather straightforward thought has had on society. *Hamlet* has also been translated into modern English by several authors; search that, as well.

Check out the best of Marvin Gaye and Jay-Z on YouTube, as well as one of the live performances of Gaye singing "What's Going On." Witness the power and controlled emotional intensity in his voice. Also, listen to other artists' interpretations of that song.

Read any Dr. Seuss book, and try to explain why his work reaches beyond the minds of young children. Start with *Horton Hears a Who!* and *The Lorax*.

Books like *Maus* (Art Spiegelman), *Number the Stars* (Lois Lowry), and *Night* (Elie Wiesel) have a lot in common with Anne Frank's story. Give them a read to find out why. Also check out *Sophie's Choice*. It's both a great film and a novel by William Styron.

Try making a list of all the songs you know that mention either drugs or alcohol. Are these substances referred to in a positive or negative light?

CHAPTER FOUR

Go to YouTube and hear Mac Lethal perform "The History of America... Told in 27 Rap Styles." It's really well done.
Michael Jackson authored an interesting book, *Moonwalk*.
Like Dr. King's "Letter from a Birmingham Jail"? Then read *The Prison Letters of Nelson Mandela*. The collection of letters was penned by the future leader of South Africa during his 10,052-day incarceration.
Intrigued by the male/female double-standard that Beyoncé and Gwen Stefani write and sing about in this chapter? Then give the lighthearted romantic-comedy *She's the Man* a chance, especially if you appreciate sports (soccer is at its core).

CHAPTER FIVE

For fans of science fiction, check out a few episodes of *Star Trek*, and judge this vehicle of the 1960s against modern sci-fi, such as the *Star Wars* series and the *Guardians of the Galaxy* films. Observe how a different era called for writers to often assign characters roles that didn't challenge the societal mores of the time. The *Star Trek* episode "Plato's Stepchildren," however, does feature the first interracial kiss on network TV.
The *Twilight Zone* series boasts an amazing episode called "To Serve Man," which is based on Damon Knight's original story. It's considered a TV classic.

CHAPTER SIX

Besides *The Grapes of Wrath*, John Steinbeck has written a treasure trove of great books. These masterpieces include *The Pearl*, *The Red Pony*, and *Of Mice and Men*. Interested specifically in the Dust Bowl, a major theme in *The Grapes of Wrath*? Check out Timothy Egan's award-winning nonfiction book *The Worst Hard Time: The Untold Story of Those Who Survived the Great American Dust Bowl*.

Bruce Springsteen's album *The Ghost of Tom Joad* includes other songs of people facing the brutal reality of nature or society. Give a listen to "Youngstown," "Sinaloa Cowboys," "The Line," and "Across the Border."

Be sure to check out Walt Whitman's *Leaves of Grass*; Robert Frost's "Mending Wall," which gives us the line "good fences make good neighbors" (ponder that for a moment); and Bob Dylan's many protest songs, including "License to Kill."

CHAPTER SEVEN

Hoopsters into LeBron might try reading Valerie Babb's *The Book of James: The Power, Politics, and Passion of LeBron* or Brian Windhorst's *LeBron, Inc.: The Making of a Billion-Dollar Athlete*.

You can also try several of the sports-themed books I've authored. These include basketball novels *Black and White* and *The Final Four*, as well as my nonfiction memoir *Streetball Is Life*.

There is a fabulous young adult book, *Becoming Muhammad Ali*, coauthored by James Patterson and Kwame Alexander and illustrated by Dawud Anyabwile.

CHAPTER EIGHT

Enjoy the music of Bob Marley? Consider reading a book by Rita Marley (his wife) and Hettie Jones, *No Woman, No Cry: My Life with Bob Marley*. It gives a different perspective on the couple's journey together, especially if you've seen the 2024 film *Bob Marley: One Love*.

If you were intrigued by Franz Kafka, consider reading *Metamorphosis and Other Stories*. It's restrained horror at its best. Correspondingly, classic Stephen King horror includes *Pet Sematary*, *It*, *Carrie*, and *The Shining*, which have all been made into films, as well.

Interested in supers? Want to one day create your own? Then you should read *A Marvelous Life: The Amazing Story of Stan Lee* by Danny Fingeroth. After all, among Lee's creations are Spider-Man, the Hulk, Iron Man, and the X-Men.

Into Batman? Read Rob Salkowitz's article "Batman's Co-Creator Bill Finger Finally Receives Recognition." It will make you think twice about sharing an artistic idea with a friend, especially without a contract.

CHAPTER NINE

Experience Shakespeare's *Romeo and Juliet* in different ways through the myriad works inspired by it. These include the martial arts-themed *Romeo Must Die*; *Gnomeo & Juliet* (are you crazy about gnomes, too?); *Romeo + Juliet* (with Leonardo DiCaprio); *Shakespeare in Love*; and the classic (and sometimes controversial) *West Side Story*, in which a pair of rival street gangs assume the place of the feuding clans.

If you admire Jane Austen's novel, give the 2005 film *Pride and Prejudice* a screening.

Moved by Janis Ian's brutally honest song "At Seventeen"? Then you really want to read an excellent interview with her conducted by Dale Kawashima, "Acclaimed Singer/Songwriter Janis Ian Talks About Her Great Career, from Her Hit 'At Seventeen' to Her New Album, *The Light at the End of the Line*." Wonderful reflection from an artist now in her sixties.

CHAPTER TEN

If you search the names of any of the orators in this chapter, you can find all their full speeches online. Also look for them on YouTube and add the power of their voices to their incredible words. This includes Dr. Martin Luther King Jr.'s final speech, "I've Been to the Mountaintop."

CHAPTER ELEVEN

Unfamiliar with the work of the Beatles? Try the albums *The Beatles* (commonly called the White Album because of its cover color), *Abbey Road*, and *Let It Be*.

If you thought Huck Finn was a cool character, read some of Mark Twain's other works, such as *The Adventures of Tom Sawyer* and the short story "The Celebrated Jumping Frog from Calaveras County." Believe it or not, that story is about betting an amount of money that matters on one frog jumping farther than another. That's what they did for fun back then.

If you found the song "Seasons of Love" to be moving, you can see most of the musical from which it hails, *Rent*, online.

Wicked was released as a film in late 2024, starring Ariana Grande (Galinda) and Cynthia Erivo (Elphaba). The second part of the film is scheduled to hit theaters in late 2025. And be sure to read Gregory Maguire's novel *Wicked: The Life and Times of the Wicked Witch of the West*. It's the sublime vehicle that spurred both the musical and the movie.

CHAPTER TWELVE

This chapter couldn't possibly be long enough to include all the great YA books out there, so here are a few more you might want to experience. *The Outsiders* (S. E. Hinton; now a Broadway musical); *Whale Talk* (Chris Crutcher); *The Life I'm In* (Sharon G. Flake); and *The Face on the Milk Carton* (Caroline B. Cooney) might make you smile—and think.

Be sure to view the full episode of *South Park*'s exploration of the kids at South Park Elementary reading *The Catcher in the Rye*. It's uniquely titled "The Tale of Scrotie McBoogerballs." No, I'm not making that up. It's true. Check it out.

CHAPTER THIRTEEN

Find out what happens when a world-renowned songwriter is forced to deal with his failing hearing in the *CBS Mornings* interview "Paul Simon on Coming to Terms with Hearing Loss, Searching for Answers." Search for it on various platforms.

So you think you want to be a star? Search for Ahmir "Questlove" Thompson's article on Bill Withers, "Questlove on Bill Withers: 'He Was True to Himself to the End,'" which explains how this songwriting and performing genius never wanted to be famous.

CHAPTER FOURTEEN

If you're a Percy Jackson fan, go to Rick Riordan's website and read an extended interview with the author, getting background on him and the series.

Go to YouTube to watch singer Grace Slick perform "White Rabbit" with the psychedelic rock band Jefferson Airplane.

Watch the film *The Princess Bride*. Then read the novel that inspired it. Which do you find more amusing? How many times between the two do you laugh out loud?

Want to know more about J. R. R. Tolkien, the writer behind *The Hobbit* and *The Lord of the Rings*? Check out a book by David Day, *An Encyclopedia of Tolkien: The History and Mythology That Inspired Tolkien's World*.

CHAPTER FIFTEEN

Mary Shelley's literary *Frankenstein* has spawned many TV and movie versions of her classic tale. Legendary horror actor Boris Karloff played the Monster on the big screen in both *Frankenstein* and *The Bride of Frankenstein*. Comedy, too? Yes, the slapstick team of Bud Abbot and Lou Costello starred beside several horror monsters in *Abbott and Costello Meet Frankenstein*. Then there's the laugh fest of actor Gene Wilder portraying Dr. Frederick Frankenstein (grandson of the original) in the Mel Brooks–directed *Young Frankenstein*. A version for kids? The animated *Frankenweenie* does the trick, with a bull terrier dog being brought back to life by the Frankenstein family via a laboratory lightning bolt. Classic TV boasted its own version with the lovable but often misunderstood Herman Munster as head of his spooky clan in *The Munsters*.

CHAPTER SIXTEEN

Author Ray Bradbury has proven to be quite a prognosticator of the future. His novel *Fahrenheit 451* is playing out across much of the United States today as school districts are under heavy pressure to ban books, even books considered classics, for often obscure reasons.

Check out Elaine McArdle's article, "Book Bans and the Librarians Who Won't Be Hushed." It's an amazingly important issue, especially if you believe in free speech.

CHAPTER SEVENTEEN

There have been times when an astounding number of people were gathered around their TVs sharing an experience, such as Neil Armstrong first setting foot on the moon. Back in 1984, it's estimated that around 60 percent of US homes were tuned into the series finale of *M*A*S*H*, ending its eleven-season run. You can view full episodes online and most likely in reruns on cable. Take a few moments, and see why it touched the lives of so many viewers.

CHAPTER EIGHTEEN

If you're a fan of *The Handmaid's Tale*, either the classic novel or the streaming series, you may want to read up on Canadian author Margaret Atwood and what moved her to create such a story. There's the outstanding Penguin Books article "Margaret Atwood on the Real-Life Events That Inspired The Handmaid's Tale and The Testaments" (the sequel).

Like dystopian themes? Want to write such a story yourself one day? Read the biography of *Hunger Games* author Suzanne Collins on her website. She actually began a writing career working on the staffs of several Nickelodeon TV shows for kids.

The reality-competition TV show *Big Brother* finds its roots in George Orwell's novel *Nineteen Eighty-Four*. Read the opening few chapters of Orwell's work, and then check out an episode or two of the TV series. It's a more-than-interesting comparison as Big Brother comes to life.

BIBLIOGRAPHY

Adams, Douglas. *The Hitchhiker's Guide to the Galaxy*. Ballantine Books, 1997.
Adele, and Greg Kurstin. "I Drink Wine." Lyrics. 2021. https://www.lyrics.com/lyric/39080103/Adele/I+Drink+Wine.
Alexander, David, dir. *Star Trek*. Season 3, episode 10, "Plato's Stepchildren." Aired November 22, 1968, on NBC.
Alexie, Sherman. "Victory." Best Poems Encyclopedia. 2015. https://100.best-poems.net/victory.html.
Anderson, T. M. *Feed*. Candlewick Press, 2002.
Angelou, Maya. "Caged Bird." Poetry Foundation. 1983. https://www.poetryfoundation.org/poems/48989/caged-bird.
Angelou, Maya. "On the Pulse of Morning." Poets.org. 1993. https://poets.org/poem/pulse-morning.
Angelou, Maya. "Phenomenal Woman." Poetry Foundation. 1978. https://www.poetryfoundation.org/poems/48985/phenomenal-woman.
Archer, Wesley, Rich Moore, and David Silverman, dirs. *The Simpsons*. Season 2, episode 3, "Treehouse of Horror." Aired October 25, 1990, on Fox.
Armstrong, Neil. "Neil Armstrong." Wikiquote. Updated November 15, 2021. https://en.wikiquote.org/wiki/Neil_Armstrong.
Armstrong, Neil. "Neil Armstrong Quotes." Brainy Quote. Accessed February 18, 2025. https://www.brainyquote.com/quotes/neil_armstrong_101138.
Asbury, Kelly, dir. *Gnomeo & Juliet*. Touchstone Pictures, 2011.
Atwood, Margaret. *The Handmaid's Tale*. Penguin Books, 1998.
Atwood, Margaret. "Margaret Atwood on How She Came to Write *The Handmaid's Tale*." Literary Hub. April 25, 2018. https://lithub.com/margaret-atwood-on-how-she-came-to-write-the-handmaids-tale/.
Austen, Jane. *Pride and Prejudice*. New American Library, 2008.
Babb, Valerie. *The Book of James: The Power, Politics and Passion of LeBron*. PublicAffairs, 2023.
Ballard, Glen, and Siedah Garrett. "Man in the Mirror." AZLyrics. 1987. https://www.azlyrics.com/lyrics/michaeljackson/maninthemirror.html.
Baraka, Amiri. "Preface to a Twenty Volume Suicide Note." Lifelong Learning Collaborative. 1961. https://www.lifelonglearningcollaborative

.org/luminous-things/assignment-calendar/preface-to-a-twenty-volume.pdf.

Bare, Richard L., dir. *Twilight Zone*. Season 3, episode 24, "To Serve Man." Aired March 2, 1962, on CBS.

Barrie, James Matthew. *Peter and Wendy*. Project Gutenberg, 2008. https://www.gutenberg.org/files/26654/26654-h/26654-h.htm.

Bartkowiak, Andrzej, dir. *Romeo Must Die*. Warner Bros., 2000.

Barton, Charles, and Walter Lantz, dirs. *Abbott and Costello Meet Frankenstein*. Universal International Pictures, 1948.

The Beatles. *Abbey Road*. Produced by George Martin. Apple Records. Released September 26, 1969.

The Beatles. *The Beatles*. Produced by George Martin. Apple Records. Released November 22, 1968.

The Beatles. *Let It Be*. Produced by Phil Spector. Apple Records. Released May 8, 1970.

Berry, Wendell. "Enemies." Poetry Foundation. 1994. https://www.poetryfoundation.org/poems/58187/enemies-56d23c5817a91.

Beyoncé. "If I Were a Boy." Lyric Advisor. 2008. https://www.streetdirectory.com/lyricadvisor/song/elaoa/if_i_were_a_boy/.

Blake, William. "The Lamb." Poetry Foundation. 1789. https://www.poetryfoundation.org/poems/43670/the-lamb-56d222765a3e1.

Blake, William. "The Tyger." Poetry Foundation. 1794. https://www.poetryfoundation.org/poems/43687/the-tyger.

Bradbury, Ray. *Fahrenheit 451*. Simon and Schuster, 2013.

Brooks, Mel. "Spaceballs (1987) Title Sequence." YouTube. Posted by MovieTitles, November 7, 2017. Video, 2 min., 1 sec. https://www.youtube.com/watch?v=Ex-_6c4tSK8.

Brooks, Mel, dir. *Young Frankenstein*. Gruskoff/Venture Films, 1974.

Browning, Elizabeth Barrett. "How Do I Love Thee? Let Me Count the Ways." Poetry Foundation. 1850. https://www.poetryfoundation.org/poems/43742/sonnets-from-the-portuguese-43-how-do-i-love-thee-let-me-count-the-ways.

Bulwar-Lytton, Edward. *Paul Clifford*. Project Gutenberg, 2018. https://www.gutenberg.org/files/7735/7735-h/7735-h.htm.

Burton, Tim, dir. *Frankenweenie*. Walt Disney Pictures, 2012.

Carroll, Lewis. *Alice's Adventures in Wonderland*. Project Gutenberg, 2024. https://www.gutenberg.org/files/11/11-h/11-h.htm.

Chernow, Ron. *Alexander Hamilton*. Penguin Books, 2004.

Chief Joseph. "I Will Fight No More Forever." Edited by Jace Weaver. Teaching American History. October 5, 1877. https://teachingamericanhistory.org/document/i-will-fight-no-more-forever/.

Collins, Suzanne. "Biography." Suzanne Collins. Accessed February 23, 2025. https://www.suzannecollinsbooks.com/bio.htm.

Collins, Suzanne. *The Hunger Games*. Scholastic, 2008.

Cooney, Caroline B. *The Face on the Milk Carton*. Bantam Books, 1990.

Coppola, Francis Ford, and Edmund North. "PATTON Introduction Speech Intro (English)." YouTube. Posted by JELIOS Jerome: Motors, Cinéma, and GeekHobbies, April 17, 2020. Video, 6 min., 10 sec. https://www.youtube.com/watch?v=PS5yfhPGaWE.

Crutcher, Chris. *Whale Talk*. Greenwillow Books, 2001.

Darabont, Frank. *The Shawshank Redemption*. Screenplay. Daily Script, 2024. https://www.dailyscript.com/scripts/shawshank.html.

David, Larry. "The Final Ending of Seinfeld." YouTube. Posted by movie aesthetics, April 3, 2017. Video, 1 min., 52 sec. https://www.youtube.com/watch?v=AfdaTWOCTnk.

David, Larry, and Jerry Seinfeld. "SEINFELD HD—Pilot First Scene." YouTube. Posted by Best Collection HD, June 8, 2017. Video, 3 min., 30 sec. https://www.youtube.com/watch?v=t78wsanjaYw.

Denver, John. *Annie's Song*, youtube.com, 2018. https://www.youtube.com/watch?v=TyJRsp5t9mA.

Dickens, Charles. *A Tale of Two Cities*. Dalmatian Press, 2007. https://archive.org/details/taleoftwocities0000unse_e2i3/page/n7/mode/2up.

Dickinson, Emily. "I Heard a Fly Buzz." Poets.org. 1896. https://poets.org/poem/i-heard-fly-buzz-465.

Dickinson, Emily. "I'm Nobody! Who Are You?" Poets.org. 1891. https://poets.org/poem/im-nobody-who-are-you-260.

Dioguardi, Kara, Alecia Moore, Nate Hills, and Marcella Araica. "Sober." AZLyrics. 2008. https://www.azlyrics.com/lyrics/pink/sober.html.

Ditko, Steve, and Stan Lee. "Spider-Man." *Amazing Fantasy* 1, no. 15 (August 15, 1962): 1–11. https://archive.org/details/Amazing_Fantasy_vol1_15_201607.

Donne, John. *Devotions upon Emergent Occasions: Together with Death's Duel*. University of Michigan Press, 1959.

Dougherty, Sean Thomas. "Biography of LeBron as Ohio." Poetry Foundation. 2018. https://www.poetryfoundation.org/poems/146907/biography-of-lebron-as-ohio.

Douglass, Frederick. *Narrative of the Life of Frederick Douglass, an American Slave*. University of North Carolina at Chapel Hill, 1999. https://docsouth.unc.edu/neh/douglass/douglass.html.

Doyle, Arthur Conan. *The Sign of the Four*. Project Gutenberg Australia, 2016. https://gutenberg.net.au/ebooks/c00018.html.

Doyle, Arthur Conan. *A Study in Scarlet*. Project Gutenberg, 2023. https://www.gutenberg.org/files/244/244-h/244-h.htm.

Dr. Seuss. *The Butter Battle Book*. Random House, 1984.

Dr. Seuss. *Horton Hears a Who!* Party ed. Random House, 2008.

Dr. Seuss. *The Lorax*. Random House, 1971.

Dylan, Bob. "Blowin' in the Wind." AZLyrics. 1962. https://www.azlyrics.com/lyrics/bobdylan/blowininthewind.html.

Dylan, Bob. "License to Kill." Genius. 1983. https://genius.com/Bob-dylan-license-to-kill-lyrics.

Egan, Timothy. *The Worst Hard Time: The Untold Story of Those Who Survived the Great American Dust Bowl*. Houghton Mifflin, 2006.

Eilish, Billie, and Finneas O'Connell. "What Was I Made For?" AZLyrics. 2023. https://www.azlyrics.com/lyrics/billieeilish/whatwasimadefor.html.

Ellison, Ralph. *Invisible Man*. Vintage International, 1995.

Ellison, Ralph. Prologue. In *Invisible Man*. Café Literario en Buenos Aires, 2018. https://cafeliterarioba.com/wp-content/uploads/2018/04/ralph-ellison-invisible-man-prologue.pdf.

Eminem. "Stan." Lyric Advisor. 2009. https://www.streetdirectory.com/lyricadvisor/song/wppppw/stan/.

Fickman, Andy, dir. *She's the Man*. Dreamworks Pictures, 2006.

Fingeroth, Danny. *A Marvelous Life: The Amazing Story of Stan Lee*. St. Martin's Press, 2019.

Fitzgerald, F. Scott. *The Great Gatsby*. Project Gutenberg, 2025. https://www.gutenberg.org/files/64317/64317-h/64317-h.htm.

Flake, Sharon G. *The Life I'm In*. Scholastic Press, 2021.

Frank, Anne. *The Diary of a Young Girl*. Definitive ed. Edited by Otto H. Frank and Mirjam Pressler. Translated by Susan Massotty. Everyman's Library, 2010.

Franklin, Ruth. "'The Lottery Letters.'" *New Yorker*, June 25, 2013. https://www.newyorker.com/books/page-turner/the-lottery-letters.

Frost, Robert. "Fire and Ice." Poets.org. 1920. https://poets.org/poem/fire-and-ice.

Frost, Robert. "Mending Wall." Poetry Foundation. 1914. https://www.poetryfoundation.org/poems/44266/mending-wall.

Frost, Robert. "The Road Not Taken." Poets.org. 1916. https://poets.org/poem/road-not-taken.

Gaye, Marvin. "What's Going On." Genius. 1971. https://genius.com/Marvin-gaye-whats-going-on-lyrics.

Gehrig, Lou. "Gehrig Delivers His Famous Speech at Yankee Stadium." YouTube. Posted by MLB, July 1, 2014. Video, 1 min. 9 sec. https://www.youtube.com/watch?v=nNLKPaThYkE.

Gelbert, Larry, creator. *M*A*S*H*. Aired 1972–1983 on CBS.

Gelbart, Larry. "M*A*S*H Pilot Episode Intro/Opening." YouTube. Posted by Apostolski, February 4, 2018. Video, 2 min., 30 sec. https://www.youtube.com/watch?v=2NWDgMpQvu8.

Gioia, Dana. "Insomnia." Poetry Foundation. 1986. https://www.poetryfoundation.org/poems/46413/insomnia-56d226489f4ed.

Goldman, William. *The Princess Bride: S. Morgenstern's Classic Tale of True Love and High Adventure, the "Good Parts" Version*. Harcourt, 2007.

Goldman, William. "Princess Bride Opening Scenes." YouTube. Posted by lsw83, August 21, 2013. Video, 1 min., 5 sec. https://www.youtube.com/watch?v=KXJYWb4y1Hc.

Green, Reinaldo Marcus, dir. *Bob Marley: One Love*. Paramount Pictures, 2024.

Groom, Winston. *Forrest Gump*. Doubleday, 1986.

Gunn, James, dir. *Guardians of the Galaxy*. Marvel Studios, 2014.

Gunn, James, dir. *Guardians of the Galaxy Vol. 2*. Marvel Studios, 2017.

Gunn, James, dir. *Guardians of the Galaxy Vol. 3*. Marvel Studios, 2023.

Haas, Ed, and Norm Liebmann, creators. *The Munsters*. Aired 1964–1966 on CBS.

Hafiz. "Even after All This Time." Goodreads. Accessed February 7, 2025. https://www.goodreads.com/quotes/60389-even-after-all-this-time-the-sun-never-says-to.

Hall, Tom T. "Ballad of Forty Dollars." Genius. 1968. https://genius.com/Tom-t-hall-ballad-of-forty-dollars-lyrics.

Hartford, John. "Gentle on My Mind." Genius. 1967. https://genius.com/Glen-campbell-gentle-on-my-mind-lyrics.

Hasford, Gustav. *The Short-Timers*. Harper & Row, 1979.

Hasford, Gustav, Michael Herr, and Stanley Kubrick. "Full Metal Jacket—Opening Scene." YouTube. Posted by P2Deerhunter, October 20,

2009. Video, 1 min., 35 sec. https://www.youtube.com/watch?v=Mw MPZR3sS2o.

Haynes, Charles. "Muhammad Ali: 'I Am America.'" Freedom Forum. August 8, 2016. https://www.freedomforum.org/i-am-america/.

Henry, Patrick. "Give Me Liberty or Give Me Death!" Colonial Williamsburg. March 3, 2020. https://www.colonialwilliamsburg.org/learn/deep-dives/give-me-liberty-or-give-me-death/.

Hinton, S. E. *The Outsiders*. Viking, 2019.

Holland, Eva. "Why We Play: Doing What We Love, Despite the Risks." SBNation. June 25, 2014. https://www.sbnation.com/longform/2014/6/25/5838366/why-we-play-doing-what-we-love-despite-the-risks.

Hughes, John. "Ferris Bueller's Day Off Opening Monologue 4K." YouTube. Posted by Movie Takedown, April 30, 2022. Video, 2 min. 47 sec. https://www.youtube.com/watch?v=Yl8atcP1BW4.

Hughes, Langston. "Mother to Son." Poetry Foundation. 2002. https://www.poetryfoundation.org/poems/47559/mother-to-son.

Hughes, Langston. "Thank You, M'am." Creative Education, 1991.

Ian, Janis. "At Seventeen." Genius. 1975. https://genius.com/Janis-ian-at-seventeen-lyrics.

Jackson, Michael. *Moonwalk*. Doubleday, 1988.

Jackson, Michael, and Lionel Richie. "We Are the World." Genius. 1985. https://genius.com/Usa-for-africa-we-are-the-world-lyrics.

Jackson, Shirley. "The Lottery." *New Yorker*, June 18, 1948. https://www.newyorker.com/magazine/1948/06/26/the-lottery.

Jay-Z, Beanie Sigel, Scarface, Just Blaze, and Michael McGloiry. "Some How Some Way." Lyric Advisor. 2009. https://www.streetdirectory.com/lyricadvisor/song/ppjlwo/some_how_some_way/.

Jefferson, Thomas, John Adams, Benjamin Franklin, Roger Sherman, and Robert R. Livingston. Declaration of Independence. National Archives. 1776. https://www.archives.gov/founding-docs/declaration-transcript.

Joel, Billy. "New Billy Joel Q&A—Can You Tell Me What Made You Write the Song 'Summer, Highland Falls'?" August 17, 2011. https://www.billyjoel.com/news/new-billy-joel-qa-can-you-tell-me-what-made-you-write-song-summer-highland-falls/.

Joel, Billy. "Summer, Highland Falls." AZLyrics. 1976. https://www.azlyrics.com/lyrics/billyjoel/summerhighlandfalls.html.

Juan-austin, Rose Marie. "Poetry Is a Solitary Art." PoemHunter.com. 2018. https://www.poemhunter.com/poem/poetry-is-a-solitary-art.

Juster, Norton. *The Phantom Tollbooth.* 50th anniversary ed. Alfred A. Knopf, 2011.

Kafka, Franz. *The Metamorphosis.* In *The Complete Stories,* 89–139. Edited by Nahum N. Glazer. Translated by Willa Muir and Edwin Muir. Schocken Books, 1971. https://www.sas.upenn.edu/~cavitch/pdf-library/Kafka_Metamorphosis.pdf.

Kafka, Franz. *The Metamorphosis and Other Stories.* Translated by Stanley Appelbaum. Dover, 2025.

Kane, Bob, and Bill Finger. "The Legend of the Batman." *Batman,* no. 1 (Spring 1940). https://archive.org/details/batman150/Batman%20001/.

Kawashima, Dale. "Acclaimed Singer/Songwriter Janis Ian Talks About Her Great Career, from Her Hit 'At Seventeen' to Her New Album, *The Light at the End of the Line.*" SongwriterUniverse. January 12, 2023. https://www.songwriteruniverse.com/janis-ian-songs-at-seventeen-light-at-the-end-of-the-line-2023.htm.

Kelly, Donika Ross. "Love Poem: Mermaid." *Pleiades: Literature in Context* 36, no. 2 (Summer 2016): 43. https://muse.jhu.edu/pub/281/article/618176/pdf.

King, Martin Luther, Jr. "Letter from a Birmingham Jail [King, Jr.]." African Studies Center, University of Pennsylvania. April 16, 1963. https://www.africa.upenn.edu/Articles_Gen/Letter_Birmingham.html.

King, Martin Luther, Jr. "Read Martin Luther King Jr.'s 'I Have a Dream' Speech in Its Entirety." NPR. Updated January 16, 2023. https://www.npr.org/2010/01/18/122701268/i-have-a-dream-speech-in-its-entirety.

King, Stephen. *Carrie.* Anchor Books, 2013.

King, Stephen. *It: A Novel.* Scribner, 2019.

King, Stephen. *On Writing: A Memoir of the Craft.* Scribner, 2000.

King, Stephen. *Pet Sematary: A Novel.* Scribner, 2018.

King, Stephen. *Rita Hayworth and the Shawshank Redemption.* Viking Press, 1982.

King, Stephen. *The Shining.* Anchor Books, 2013.

Kinney, Jeff. *Diary of a Wimpy Kid.* Amulet, 2007.

Knight, Damon. "To Serve Man." *Galaxy Science Fiction,* November 1950.

Knopfler, Mark. "Romeo and Juliet." AZLyrics. 1980. https://www.azlyrics.com/lyrics/direstraits/romeoandjuliet.html.

Kubrick, Stanley, and Arthur C. Clark. *2001: A Space Odyssey.* Screenplay. Archivio Kubrick. 1968. http://www.archiviokubrick.it/opere/film/2001/script/2001-originalscript.pdf.

Larson, Jonathan. "Seasons of Love." Genius. 1996. https://genius.com/Original-broadway-cast-of-rent-seasons-of-love-lyrics.

L'Engle, Madeleine. *A Wrinkle in Time.* Ariel Books, 1962.

Lennon, John, and Yoko Ono. "Imagine." AZLyrics. 1971. https://www.azlyrics.com/lyrics/johnlennon/imagine.html.

Lennon–McCartney. "Yesterday." Genius. 1965. https://genius.com/The-beatles-yesterday-lyrics.

Levertov, Denise. "Making Peace." Poetry Foundation. 1987. https://www.poetryfoundation.org/poems/53900/making-peace.

Limón, Ada. "Notes on the Below." Poets.org. 2016. https://poets.org/poem/notes-below.

Lincoln, Abraham. "The Gettysburg Address." Abraham Lincoln Online. November 19, 1863. https://www.abrahamlincolnonline.org/lincoln/speeches/gettysburg.htm.

Little, Joel, and Ella Yelich-O'Connor. "Royals." AZLyrics. 2013. https://www.azlyrics.com/lyrics/lorde/royals.html.

Lowry, Lois. *Number the Stars.* Houghton Mifflin Harcourt, 2014.

Lucas, George. "Star Wars Intro HD 1080p." YouTube. Posted by Greg, August 4, 2010. Video, 1 min., 28 sec. https://www.youtube.com/watch?v=tGsKzZtRwxw.

Luhrmann, Baz, dir. *Romeo + Juliet.* Twentieth Century Fox, 1996.

Madden, John, dir. *Shakespeare in Love.* Universal Pictures, 1998.

Maguire, Gregory. *Wicked: The Life and Times of the Wicked Witch of the West: A Novel.* ReganBooks, 1995.

Mandela, Nelson. *The Prison Letters of Nelson Mandela.* Edited by Sahm Venter. Liveright, 2018.

Marley, Bob. "Redemption Song." AZLyrics. 1980. https://www.azlyrics.com/lyrics/bobmarley/redemptionsong.html.

Marley, Rita, and Hettie Jones. *No Woman, No Cry: My Life with Bob Marley.* Hyperion, 2004.

Marston, William Moulton. "Introducing Wonder Woman." *All-Star Comics*, no. 8 (December 1941–January 1942): 2–10. https://archive.org/details/wonderwomanarchi0000mars/page/n19/mode/2up.

McArdle, Elaine. "Book Bans the Librarians Who Won't Be Hushed." Harvard Graduate School of Education. November 6, 2023. https://www.gse.harvard.edu/ideas/ed-magazine/23/11/book-bans-and-librarians-who-wont-be-hushed.

McCullah, Karen, and Kristen Smith. "10 Things I Hate about You—Full Poem Scene HD." YouTube. Posted by ThatVideoGirl1997,

August 13, 2013. Video, 1 min., 44 sec. https://www.youtube.com/watch?v=31N_HM2f9Ks.
McKay, Jim. "ABC's Wide World of Sports Opening 1976 4k." YouTube. Posted by Television Archives, July 31, 2023. Video, 1 min., 7 sec. https://www.youtube.com/watch?v=SnakqX0pTUk.
McLean, Don. "Vincent (Starry, Starry Night)." Lyric Advisor. 1972. https://www.streetdirectory.com/lyricadvisor/song/cojafp/vincent_starry_starry_night/.
Melville, Herman. *Moby-Dick; or, The Whale.* Harper & Brothers, 1851. https://melville.electroniclibrary.org/editions/versions-of-moby-dick/front-matter.
Meyer, Stephenie. *Twilight.* Little, Brown, 2005. https://www.sausd.us/cms/lib/CA01000471/Centricity/Domain/241/1-stephenie-meyer-twilight.pdf.
Miranda, Lin-Manuel. "Alexander Hamilton." Genius. 2015. https://genius.com/Leslie-odom-jr-anthony-ramos-daveed-diggs-okieriete-onaodowan-lin-manuel-miranda-phillipa-soo-christopher-jackson-and-original-broadway-cast-of-hamilton-alexander-hamilton-lyrics.
Nigro, Dan, Casey Smith, and Olivia Rodrigo. "Jealousy, Jealousy." AZLyrics. 2021. https://genius.com/Olivia-rodrigo-jealousy-jealousy-lyrics.
Odom, Selena. "My Master." Family Friend Poems. August 13, 2010. https://www.familyfriendpoems.com/poem/my-master.
Orlean, Susan. "Life's Swell." Outside. August 23, 2002. https://www.outsideonline.com/outdoor-adventure/water-activities/lifes-swell/.
Orwell, George. *Nineteen Eighty-Four.* Penguin Classics, 2013.
Page, James Patrick, and Robert Plant. "Stairway to Heaven." AZ Lyrics. 1971. https://www.azlyrics.com/lyrics/ledzeppelin/stairwaytoheaven.html.
Parker, Trey, dir. *South Park.* Season 14, episode 2, "The Tale of Scrotie McBoogerballs." Aired March 24, 2010, on Comedy Central.
Patterson, James, and Kwame Alexander. *Becoming Muhammad Ali: A Novel.* Little, Brown, 2020.
Paulson, Michael. "'Hamilton' Heads to Broadway in a Hip-Hop Retelling." *New York Times,* July 12, 2015. https://www.nytimes.com/2015/07/13/theater/hamilton-heads-to-broadway-in-a-hip-hop-retelling.html.
Paz, Octavio. "The Street." Translated by Muriel Rukeyser. All Poetry. 1963. https://allpoetry.com/The--Street-.

Penguin Books. "Margaret Atwood on the Real-Life Events That Inspired The Handmaid's Tale and The Testaments." September 9, 2019. https://www.penguin.co.uk/discover/articles/margaret-atwood-handmaids-tale-testaments-real-life-inspiration.

Pilkey, Dav. "Captain Underpants: The First Epic Movie—Opening Scene." YouTube. Posted by Veggieboy Ultimate, June 11, 2023. Video, 4 min., 12 sec. https://www.youtube.com/watch?v=OCf_WbMBcUM&t=62s.

Poe, Edgar Allan. "The Raven." Poetry Foundation. 1845. https://www.poetryfoundation.org/poems/48860/the-raven.

Prine, John. "Sam Stone." Genius. 1971. https://genius.com/John-prine-sam-stone-lyrics.

Reiner, Rob, dir. *The Princess Bride*. Buttercup Films, 1987.

Riordan, Rick. "An Interview with Rick." Rick Riordan. Accessed February 23, 2025. https://rickriordan.com/about/an-interview-with-rick/.

Riordan, Rick. *The Lightning Thief*. Percy Jackson and the Olympians. Penguin Books, 2013.

Roddenberry, Gene. "Star Trek: The Next Generation Intro HD." YouTube. Posted by Eric Whalen, January 31, 2012. Video, 1 min., 46 sec. https://www.youtube.com/watch?v=HnDtvZXYHgE.

Roddenberry, Gene. "Star Trek Original Series Intro (HQ)." YouTube. Posted by dinadangdong, July 23, 2007. Video, 57 sec. https://www.youtube.com/watch?v=hdjL8WXjlGI.

Ronson, Mark, and Amy Winehouse. "Rehab." Genius. 2006. https://genius.com/Amy-winehouse-rehab-lyrics.

Rose, Reginald. *Twelve Angry Men*. Stage version by Sherman L. Sergel. Dramatic, 1955. https://www.umass.edu/legal/Hilbink/250/12Angry.pdf.

Roth, Eric. *Forrest Gump* (screenplay). Daily Script. 1994. https://www.dailyscript.com/scripts/forrest_gump.html.

Roth, Veronica. *Divergent*. Katherine Tegen Books, 2011.

Rowling, J. K. *Harry Potter and the Philosopher's Stone*. Bloomsbury, 1997.

Salinger, J. D. *The Catcher in the Rye*. Little, Brown, 1951.

Salkowitz, Rob. "Batman's Co-Creator Bill Finger Finally Receives Recognition." *Forbes*, September 19, 2015. https://www.forbes.com/sites/robsalkowitz/2015/09/19/batmans-co-creator-bill-finger-finally-receives-recognition/.

Schulz, Charles M. *It Was a Dark and Stormy Night, Snoopy*. Ballantine Books, 2004.

Schulz, Charles M. *Snoopy and "It Was a Dark and Stormy Night."* Holt, Rinehart and Winston, 1971.

Schwartz, Stephen. "What Is This Feeling?" Genius. 2003. https://genius.com/Kristin-chenoweth-and-idina-menzel-what-is-this-feeling-lyrics.

Shakespeare, William. Sonnet 18: Shall I compare thee to a summer's day? Poetry Foundation. 1609. https://www.poetryfoundation.org/poems/45087/sonnet-18-shall-i-compare-thee-to-a-summers-day.

Shakespeare, William. *The Tragedy of Hamlet, Prince of Denmark.* Edited by Barbara A. Mowat and Paul Werstine. Simon & Schuster, 2012.

Shakespeare, William. *The Tragedy of Macbeth.* Edited by Barbara A. Mowat and Paul Werstine. Simon & Schuster, 2013.

Shakespeare, William. *The Tragedy of Romeo and Juliet.* Edited by Barbara A. Mowat and Paul Werstine. Simon & Schuster, 2011.

Shellback, Max Martin, and Taylor Swift. "Blank Space." Genius. 2014. https://genius.com/Taylor-swift-blank-space-lyrics.

Shelley, Mary. *Frankenstein: Or, The Modern Prometheus.* Henry Colburn and Richard Bentley, 1831. https://www.gutenberg.org/files/42324/42324-h/42324-h.htm.

Siegel, Jerome, and Joe Shuster. "Superman." *Action Comics*, no. 1 (1938): 1–13.

Simon, Paul. "Extended Interview: Paul Simon on Coming to Terms with Hearing Loss, Searching for Answers." YouTube. Posted by CBS, November 21, 2024. Video, 15 min., 46 sec. https://www.youtube.com/watch?v=H5wdvaBAPaM.

Simon, Paul. "The Sound of Silence." Genius. 1964. https://genius.com/Simon-and-garfunkel-the-sound-of-silence-lyrics.

Slick, Grace Wing. "White Rabbit." AZLyrics. 1967. https://www.azlyrics.com/lyrics/jeffersonairplane/whiterabbit.html.

Smith, Betty. *A Tree Grows in Brooklyn.* Harper & Brothers, 1943.

Snicket, Lemony [Daniel Handler]. *The Bad Beginning.* A Series of Unfortunate Events, no. 1. HarperCollins, 1999.

Sobol, Donald J. *Encyclopedia Brown Gets His Man.* Lodestar Books, 1967. https://archive.org/details/encyclopediabget00sobo/page/n7/mode/2up.

Spiegelman, Art. *Maus: A Survivor's Tale.* Pantheon Books, 1986.

Spielberg, Steven. *West Side Story.* 20th Century Studios, 2021.

Springsteen, Bruce. *The Ghost of Tom Joad.* Produced by Bruce Springsteen and Chuck Plotkin. Columbia Records. Released November 21, 1995.

Springsteen, Bruce. "The Ghost of Tom Joad." AZLyrics. 1995. https://www.azlyrics.com/lyrics/brucespringsteen/theghostoftomjoad.html.

Stefani, Gwen, and Tom Dumont. "I'm Just a Girl." Lyrics.com. 1997. https://www.lyrics.com/lyric/1695886/No+Doubt.

Steinbeck, John. *The Grapes of Wrath*. Viking, 1939.

Steinbeck, John. *Of Mice and Men*. Penguin Books, 1994.

Steinbeck, John. *The Pearl*. Penguin Books, 2002.

Steinbeck, John. *The Red Pony*. Penguin Books, 1994.

Strand, Mark. "Eating Poetry." Poets.org. 2014. https://poets.org/poem/eating-poetry.

Stump, Andrew. "Tolkien's 1965 Interview." Quora. 2019. https://tolkienbystump.quora.com/Tolkien-s-1965-Interview.

Styron, William. *Sophie's Choice*. Random House, 1979.

Swift, Taylor, Max Martin, and Shellback. "I Knew You Were Trouble (Taylor's Version)." Genius. 2021. https://genius.com/Taylor-swift-i-knew-you-were-trouble-taylors-version-lyrics.

Taupin, Bernie, and Elton John. "Candle in the Wind." AZLyrics. 1973. https://www.azlyrics.com/lyrics/eltonjohn/candleinthewind.html.

Taupin, Bernie, and Elton John. "Candle in the Wind 1997." Genius. 1997. https://genius.com/Elton-john-candle-in-the-wind-1997-lyrics.

Thayer, Ernest Lawrence. "Casey at the Bat." Poets.org. 1888. https://poets.org/poem/casey-bat.

Thomas, Dylan. "Do Not Go Gentle into That Good Night." Poetry Foundation. 1939. https://www.poetryfoundation.org/poems/46569/do-not-go-gentle-into-that-good-night.

Thompson, Ahmir "Questlove." "Questlove on Bill Withers: 'He Was True to Himself to the End.'" *Rolling Stone*, April 9, 2020. https://www.rollingstone.com/music/music-features/questlove-bill-withers-tribute-my-idol-980709/.

Thunberg, Greta. "Transcript: Greta Thunberg's Speech at the U.N. Climate Action Summit." NPR. September 23, 2019. https://www.npr.org/2019/09/23/763452863/transcript-greta-thunbergs-speech-at-the-u-n-climate-action-summit.

Tolkien, J. R. R. *The Hobbit, or, There and Back Again*. Houghton Mifflin, 2001.

Tolkien, J. R. R. *The Lord of the Rings*. Houghton Mifflin, 2001.

Turner, Brian. "The Hurt Locker." Poetry Foundation. 2005. https://www.poetryfoundation.org/poems/54141/the-hurt-locker.

Twain, Mark. *The Adventures of Huckleberry Finn*. Puffin Books, 2018.
Twain, Mark. *The Adventures of Tom Sawyer*. Canon Press, 2019.
Twain, Mark. *The Celebrated Jumping Frog of Calaveras County, and Other Stories*. Running Press, 1989.
Uitti, Jacob. "The 13 Best Bill Withers Quotes." American Songwriter. March 15, 2023. https://americansongwriter.com/the-13-best-bill-withers-quotes/.
Updike, John. "Ex-Basketball Player." Poetry Foundation. 1993. https://www.poetryfoundation.org/poems/43489/ex-basketball-player.
Vitale, Tom. "Ralph Ellison: No Longer the 'Invisible Man' 100 Years After His Birth." NPR. May 30, 2014. https://www.npr.org/sections/codeswitch/2014/05/30/317056807/ralph-ellison-no-longer-the-invisible-man-100-years-after-his-birth.
Volponi, Paul. *Black and White*. Viking, 2005.
Volponi, Paul. *The Final Four*. Viking, 2012.
Volponi, Paul. *Streetball Is Life: Lessons Earned on the Asphalt*. Rowman & Littlefield, 2020.
Welch, Willy. "Right Field." Genius. 1993. https://genius.com/Peter-paul-and-mary-right-field-live-lyrics.
Wells, H. G. *Invisible Man*. Edited by David Lake. Oxford University Press, 1996.
Wells, H. G. *The War of the Worlds*. Dover, 1997.
Wells, H. G. "War of the Worlds—Original 1938 Radio Broadcasts (2011 Remastered Version)." YouTube. Posted by Orson Welles—Topic, February 24, 2015. Video, 59 min., 17 sec. https://www.youtube.com/watch?v=9q7tN7MhQ4I.
Whale, James, dir. *The Bride of Frankenstein*. Universal Pictures, 1931.
Whale, James, dir. *Frankenstein*. Universal Pictures, 1931.
Whitfield, Norman, and Barrett Strong. "War." TeachRock.org. 1970. https://teachrock.org/wp-content/uploads/L046H02.pdf?x20857.
Whitman, Walt. *Leaves of Grass*. Folcroft Library Editions, 1975.
Whitman, Walt. "Song of the Open Road, 4." Poets.org. 1856. https://poets.org/poem/song-open-road-4.
Wiesel, Elie. *Night*. Translated by Marion Wiesel. Hill and Wang, 2017.
Williams, William Carlos. "Smell!" Poets.org. 1917. https://poets.org/poem/smell.
Windhorst, Brian. *LeBron, Inc.: The Making of a Billion-Dollar Athlete*. Grand Central, 2019.

Withers, Bill. "Lean on Me." Genius. 1972. https://genius.com/Bill-withers-lean-on-me-lyrics.

Wright, Joe, dir. *Pride & Prejudice*. Universal Pictures, 2005.

Wright, Judith. "Five Senses." All Poetry. 1963. https://allpoetry.com/Five-Senses.

Young, Neil. "The Needle and the Damage Done." Lyrics on Demand. 1972. https://mail.lyricsondemand.com/neil_young/the_needle_and_the_damage_done/video.

Yousafzai, Malala. "UN Speech on Youth Education—July 12, 2013." Iowa State University, Archives of Women's Political Communication." July 12, 2013. https://awpc.cattcenter.iastate.edu/2018/03/05/un-speech-on-youth-education-july-12-2013/.

Zemekis, Robert, dir. *Forrest Gump*. Paramount Pictures, 1993.

INDEX

Adams, Douglas, 41–42
Adams, John, 93
Adele, 49–50
Adventures of Huckleberry Finn, 105–106
Alexander Hamilton, 29
Alexie, Sherman, 63
Ali, Muhammad, 61–62, 194
Alice's Adventures in Wonderland, 140–141
Anderson, T. M., 120–121
Angelou, Maya, 9, 71–72, 192
"Annie's Song," 129–130
Armstrong, Neil, 38, 120, 198
"At Seventeen," 87–88
Atwood, Margaret, 179–180, 198
Austen, Jane, 85–86, 195

"Ballad of Forty Dollars," 157–158
Baraka, Amiri, 107–108
Barbie (film), 8
Barrie, J. M., 114–115
Baum, L. Frank, 108–109
Beatles, 101–102, 195
Berry, Wendell, 34
"Biography of LeBron as Ohio," 54–56
Blake, William, 147–149
"Blank Space," 7–8
"Blowin' in the Wind," 52
Book of Genesis, 11, 147

Bradbury, Ray, 168–169, 197
Brooks, Mel, 40, 197
Brown, Charlie, 1
Browning, Elizabeth Barrett, 88–89
Bulwar-Lytton, Edward, 2
The Butter Battle Book, 22

"Caged Bird," 71–72
Cameron, James, 182–183
"Candle in the Wind," 166–167
Captain Ahab, 11
Captain James Tiberius Kirk, 37
Captain Underpants: The First Epic Movie, 117–118
Carroll, Lewis, 140–141
Carter, Shawn (Jay–Z), 20–21, 192
"Casey at the Bat," 58–60, 65
The Catcher in the Rye, 116
Chernow, Ron, 29
Chief Joseph, 96–97
Churchill, Winston, 91
Clarke, Arthur C., 40–41
Collins, Suzanne, 181–182, 198
Coppola, Francis Ford, 176–177
Curious George, 12

Darabont, Frank, 72–73
David, Larry, 135
Declaration of Independence, 93
Denver, John, 129–130

Devotions upon Emergent Occasions, 133–134
Diary of a Wimpy Kid, 119–120
The Diary of a Young Girl, 25
Dickens, Charles, 103–104, 116
Dickinson, Emily, 15, 156–157, 192
Ditko, Steve, 77
Divergent, 184–185
"Do Not Go Gentle into That Good Night," 155–156
Donne, John, 133–134
Dougherty, Sean Thomas, 54–56
Douglass, Frederick, 163–164
Doyle, Arthur Conan, 77–78
Dumont, Tom, 35
Dylan, Bob (Robert Zimmerman), 51–52, 155, 194

"Eating Poetry," 125–126
Eilish, Billie, 8, 191–192
Ellison, Ralph, 13–14, 192
Encyclopedia Brown Gets His Man, 79
"Enemies," 34
"Ex-Basketball Player," 56–57

Fahrenheit 451, 169, 197
Feed, 120–121
Ferris Bueller's Day Off, 116–117
Finger, Bill, 75–76, 195
"Fire and Ice," 158–159
"Five Senses," 128–129
Fleming, Ian xiii
Forrest Gump, 12, 192
Frank, Anne, 24
Frankenstein; Or, The Modern Prometheus, 149–150, 197

Frost, Robert, 48–50, 158–159, 194
Full Metal Jacket, 172–173

Gaye, Marvin, 19–20, 192
Gehrig, Lou, 98–99
Geisel, Theodore (Dr. Seuss), 22, 192
Gelbart, Larry, 172–173
"Gentle on My Mind," 84–85
Gettysburg Address, 91–92, 95
The Ghost of Tom Joad, 46–47
Gioia, Dana, 154–155
Goldman, William, 142
The Grapes of Wrath, 45–47, 193
The Great Gatsby, 161–162
Groom, Winston, 12

Hafiz, 130–131
Hall, Tom T., 157–158
Hamilton, 29–30
Handler, Daniel (Lemony Snicket), 113–114
The Handmaid's Tale, 179–180, 198
Harry Potter and the Philosopher's Stone, 118–119
Hartford, John, 84–85
Hasford, Gustav, 171–172
Henry, Patrick, 93–94
Herr, Michael, 171–172
The Hitchhiker's Guide to the Galaxy, 41–42
The Hobbit, 143–144, 197
Holden Caulfield, 116
Holland, Eva, 60–61
Hornberger, H. Richard (Richard Hooker), 172–173
"How Do I Love Thee?," 88–89
Hughes, John, 116–117

Hughes, Langston, 73–74, 165
The Hunger Games, 181–182, 198
The Hurt Locker, 174–175

"I Am America," 61–62
"I Drink Wine," 49–50
"I Have a Dream," 95–97
"I Heard a Fly Buzz," 156–157
"I Knew You Were Trouble," 83–84
Ian, Janis, 87–88, 195
"If I Were a Boy," 35–36
"I'm Just a Girl," 35
"I'm Nobody! Who Are You?," 15
"Imagine," 101–102
"In the Penal Colony," 70–71
"Insomnia," 154–155
Invisible Man, 13–14, 192

Jackson, Michael, 31–32
Jackson, Shirley, 22–24
James, LeBron, 54–56, 194
James Bond (007), xiii
"Jealousy, Jealousy," 9
Jefferson, Thomas, 93
Joel, Billy, 104–105
John, Elton, 166–167
Juan-austin, Rose Marie, 131–132
Juster, Norton, 138–139

Kafka, Franz, 69–71, 194
Kane, Bob, 75–76
Kelly, Donika Ross, 86–87
King, Martin Luther, Jr., 29, 33, 95–97, 193, 195
King, Stephen, 26, 72–23, 194
Kinney, Jeff, 119–120
Knight, Damon, 42–43, 193
Knopfler, Mark, 82

Knowles-Carter, Beyoncé, 35–36, 193
Kubrick, Stanley, 40–41, 171–172
Kurstin, Greg, 49–50

La Bohème, 110
Larson, Jonathan, 110–111
Lean on Me, 133
Lee, Stan, 77, 194
L'Engle, Madeleine, 2
Lennon, John, 101–102
"Letter from a Birmingham Jail," 33
Levertov, Denise, 174
"Life's Swell," 57–58
The Lightning Thief, 139–140
Limón, Ada, 150–151
Lincoln, Abraham, 91–92, 95
The Lord of the Rings, 144–145, 197
Lorde (Ella Marija Lani Yelich-O'Connor), 162–163
The Lottery, 22–24
"Love Poem: Mermaid," 86–87
Lucas, George, 38–40

Maguire, Gregory, 108–109
"Making Peace," 174
"Man in the Mirror," 31
Marley, Bob, 69, 194
Marston, Dr. William Moulton, 76
M*A*S*H, 172–173, 198
MASH: A Novel about Three Army Doctors, 172–173
Mathers, Marshall III (Eminem), 167–168
McCartney, Paul 101–103
McCullah, Karen, 89
McKay, Jim, 53–54

McLean, Don, 4–5, 191
Melville, Herman, 11, 192
The Metamorphosis, 70–71
Meyer, Stephenie, 137–138
Miranda, Lin-Manuel, 29–30
Moby-Dick, 11, 192
Monroe, Marilyn (Norma Jeane Mortenson), 167
Moore, Alecia (Pink), 25
"Mother to Son," 165
"My Master," 26

Narrative of the Life of Frederick Douglass, an American Slave, 163–164
Nineteen Eighty-Four, 183–184, 198
North, Edmund, 176–177
"Notes on the Below," 150–151

O'Connell, Finneas, 8
Odom, Selena, 26
Orlean, Susan, 57–58
Orwell, George, 183–184, 198

Page, Jimmy, 164
Patton, 176–177
Paul Clifford, 2
Paz, Octavio, 47–48
Peanuts, 1
Peter and Wendy, 114–115
The Phantom Tollbooth, 138–139
"Phenomenal Woman," 10
Pilkey, Dav, 117–118
Plant, Robert, 164
Poe, Edgar Allan, 3–4, 14, 25, 191
"Poetry Is a Solitary Art," 131–132

"Preface to a Twenty Volume Suicide Note," 107–108
Pride and Prejudice, 85–86
Prince Hamlet, 18–19
The Princess Bride, 141–143, 197
The Princess Bride: S. Morgenstern's Classic Tale of True Love and High Adventure, The "Good Parts" Version, 141–143
Princess Diana, 167
Prine, John, 175–176

"The Raven," 3–4, 191
Ray, H. A., 12
"Redemption Song," 69
"Rehab," 26
Rent, 110–111, 196
Richie, Lionel, 31–32
Ride, Sally, 38
"Right Field," 62
Riordan, Rick, 139–140, 197
Rita Hayworth and Shawshank Redemption, 72–73
"The Road Not Taken," 48–49
Roddenberry, Gene, 37
Rodrigo, Olivia, 9, 191–192
"Romeo and Juliet" (song), 82–83
Rose, Reginald, 67–68
Ross, Stanley Ralph, 53–54
Roth, Eric, 12
Roth, Veronica, 184–185
Rowling, J. K., 118–119
"Royals," 162–163

Salinger, J. D., 116
"Sam Stone," 175–176
Schulz, Charles, 1, 191
Schwartz, Stephen, 108–109

INDEX

"Seasons of Love," 110–111, 196
Seinfeld, 134
Seinfeld, Jerry, 134
A Series of Unfortunate Events, 113–114
Serling, Rod, 43
Shakespeare, William, 17–19, 65, 81–84, 152–154, 192, 195
The Shawshank Redemption, 72–73
Shelley, Mary, 149–150, 197
Sherlock Holmes, 78
The Short-Timers, 171–172
Shuster, Joe, 75
Siegel, Jerome, 75
The Sign of the Four, 78
Simon, Paul, 126–127, 196
The Simpsons, 4, 191
Slick, Grace, 141, 197
"Smell!," 127–128
Smith, Betty, 21
Smith, Kristen, 89
Snoopy, 1, 65, 191
Snoopy and "It Was a Dark and Stormy Night," 191
"Sober," 25
Sobol, Donald, 78–79
"Some How Some Way," 20–21
"Song of the Open Road," 50–51
Songs of Experience, 147–149
Songs of Innocence, 147–149
Sonnet 18 ("Shall I Compare Thee to a Summer's Day"), 152
"The Sound of Silence," 126–127
Spaceballs, 40
Spider-Man, 77
Springsteen, Bruce, 46–47, 194
"Stairway to Heaven," 164–165
"Stan," 167–168

Star Trek, 37–38, 193
Star Trek: The Next Generation, 37
Star Wars, 38–40, 193
The Starry Night, 4–5, 191
Stefani, Gwen, 35, 193
Steinbeck, John, 45–47, 193
Strand, Mark, 125–126
Stratemeyer, Edward, 79
"The Street," 47–48
Strong, Barrett, 173
A Study in Scarlet, 78
"Summer, Highland Falls," 104–105
Superman, 75
Swift, Taylor, 7–8, 83–84, 191–192

A Tale of Two Cities, 103–104
The Taming of the Shrew, 89
Taupin, Bernie, 166–167
The Tempest, 84
10 Things I Hate about You, 89, 123
Terminator 2: Judgment Day, 182–183
"Thank You, M'am," 73–74
Thayer, Ernest Lawrence, 58–60
Thomas, Dylan, 155–156
Thunberg, Greta, 97–98
To Serve Man, 42–43
Tolkien, John Ronald Reuel, 143–145, 197
Tolstoy, Leo, 2
Tom Joad, 45–47
The Tragedy of Hamlet, Prince of Denmark, 18
The Tragedy of Macbeth, 152–154
The Tragedy of Romeo and Juliet, 81–82
A Tree Grows in Brooklyn, 21

"Treehouse of Horror," 4, 191
Turner, Brian, 174–175
Twain, Mark (Samuel Clemens), 105–106, 195–196
Twelve Angry Men, 67–68
Twilight, 137–138
The Twilight Zone, 42–43, 193
2001: A Space Odyssey, 40–41

Updike, John, 56–57
U2, 149

Van Gogh, Vincent, 4–5, 191
"Victory," 63
"Vincent," 4–5, 191

"War," 173
War and Peace, 2
The War of the Worlds, 43
"We Are the World," 31–32
Welch, Willy, 62
Wells, H. G., 43–44, 192
"What Is This Feeling?," 108–109

"What Was I Made For?," 8
"What's Going On," 19–20, 192
"White Rabbit," 141
Whitfield, Norman, 173
Whitman, Walt, 50–51, 194
Wicked, 108–109, 196
Wicked: The Life and Times of the Wicked Witch of the West, 108–109, 196
Wisher, William, 182–183
Withers, Bill, 132–133, 196
"Why We Play," 60–61
Wide World of Sports, 53–54
Williams, William Carlos, 127–128
Winehouse, Amy, 26
Wonder Woman, 76
The Wonderful Wizard of Oz, 108–109
Wright, Judith, 128–129
A Wrinkle in Time, 2

"Yesterday," 102–103
Yousafzai, Malala, 94

ABOUT THE AUTHOR

Paul Volponi is the multi-award-winning, best-selling author of more than twenty books, mostly for young adults. His novels *Black and White*, *The Final Four*, *Rikers High*, and *Top Prospect* have become staples in high school and middle school English classes across the country. Paul is also the author of several student-cherished nonfiction books published by Rowman & Littlefield, including *That's My Team: The History, Science, and Fun Behind Sports Teams' Names*; *The Great G.O.A.T. Debate: The Best of the Best in Everything from Sports to Science*; *Superhero Smart: Real-World Facts behind Comic Book Characters*; and *SpongeBob SquarePants: The Unauthorized Fun-ography*.